JUL 0 2 2015

# silence

## THE POWER OF QUIET
## IN A WORLD FULL OF NOISE

## THICH NHAT HANH

HarperOne
*An Imprint of* HarperCollins*Publishers*

HarperOne

FIRST EDITION

*Designed by Level C*

Library of Congress Cataloging-in-Publication Data is available upon request.

ISBN 978–0–06–222469–9

15 16 17 18 19   RRD(H)   10 9 8 7 6 5 4 3 2 1

# contents

silence

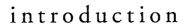

introduction

We spend a lot of time looking for happiness when the world right around us is full of wonder. To be alive and walk on the Earth is a miracle, and yet most of us are running as if there were some better place to get to. There is beauty calling to us every day, every hour, but we are rarely in a position to listen.

The basic condition for us to be able to hear the call of beauty and respond to it is silence. If we don't have silence in ourselves—if our mind, our body, are full of noise—then we can't hear beauty's call.

There's a radio playing in our head, Radio Station NST: Non-Stop Thinking. Our mind is filled with noise, and that's why we can't hear the call of life, the call of love. Our heart is calling us, but we don't hear. We don't have the time to listen to our heart.

Mindfulness is the practice that quiets the noise inside us. Without mindfulness, we can be pulled away by many things. Sometimes we are pulled away by regret and sorrow concerning the past. We revisit old memories and experiences, only to suffer again and again the pain we've already experienced. It's easy to get caught in the prison of the past.

We may also get pulled away by the future. A person who is anxious and fearful about the future is trapped just as much as one bound by the past. Anxiety, fear, and uncertainty about future events prevent us from hearing the call of happiness. So the future becomes a kind of prison, too.

Even if we try to be in the present moment, many of us are distracted and feel empty, as if we had a vacuum inside. We may long for something, expect something, wait for something to arrive to make our lives a little bit more exciting. We anticipate something that will change the situation, because we see the situation in the present moment as boring—nothing special, nothing interesting.

Mindfulness is often described as a bell that reminds us to stop and silently listen. We can use an actual bell or any other cue that helps us remember not to be carried away by the noise around and inside us. When we hear the bell, we stop. We follow our in-breath and our out-breath, making space for silence. We say to ourselves, "Breathing in, I know I'm breathing in." Breathing in and out mindfully, paying attention only to the breath, we can quiet all the noise within us—the chattering about the past, the future, and the longing for something more.

In just two or three seconds of breathing mindfully, we can awaken to the fact that we're alive, we're breathing in. We are here. We exist. The noise within just disappears and there is a profound spaciousness— it's very powerful, very eloquent. We can respond to the call of the beauty around us: "I am here. I am free. I hear you."

What does "I am here" mean? It means, "I exist. I'm really here, because I'm not lost in the past, in the future, in my thinking, in the noise inside, in the noise outside. I'm here." In order to really *be*, you have to be free from the thinking, free from the anxieties, free from the fear, free from the longing. "I am free" is a strong statement, because the truth is, many of us are not free. We don't have the freedom that allows us to hear, and to see, and to just be.

# being silent together

I live in a retreat center in southwest France where we practice a kind of silence called noble silence. The practice is easy. If we are talking, we are talking. But if we are doing something else—such as eating, walking, or working—then we do *just* these things. We aren't doing these things and also talking. So we do these things in joyful noble silence. In this way, we are free to hear the deepest call of our hearts.

Recently, there was a day when a lot of us, both monastics and laypeople, were having lunch together outside, sitting on the grass. All of us went to serve ourselves and then joined the group to sit down. We sat in concentric circles, one small circle within a larger circle, and then another, still-larger circle. We didn't say anything.

I was the first to sit down. I sat and practiced mindful breathing to establish silence in myself. I listened to the birds, to the wind, and enjoyed the beauty of spring. I wasn't waiting for others to come and sit down so I could begin eating. I just enjoyed sitting there for about twenty minutes or more, while other people served themselves and came and sat down.

There was silence. But I felt that silence was not as deep as it could have been, perhaps because people had been distracted while getting their food, walking as they held their plates, and then sitting down. I sat in silence and observed this.

I had a small bell with me, and when everyone was seated, I invited the bell to sound. Since we'd just spent a week together practicing listening to the bell and breathing in and out mindfully, we all listened very well. Right after the first sound of the bell of mindfulness, the silence felt quite different. It was real silence, because everyone had stopped thinking. We focused our attention on the in-breath as we breathed in, on the out-breath as we breathed out. We breathed together, and our collective silence generated a strong field of energy. Silence like this can be called thundering silence, because it's eloquent and powerful. In this silence, I could hear the wind and the birds so much more vividly. Before that, I'd heard the birds and the wind, but not in the same way, because I didn't have the deepest kind of silence.

Practicing silence to empty all kinds of noise within you is not a difficult practice. With some training, you can do it. In noble silence, you can walk, you can sit, you can enjoy your meal. When you have that kind of silence, you have enough freedom to enjoy being alive and to appreciate all the wonders of life. With that kind of silence you are more capable of healing yourself, mentally and physically. You have the capacity to *be,* to be there, alive. Because you really are free—free from your regrets and suffering concerning the past, free from your fear and uncertainty about the future, free from all kinds of mental chatter. Being silent in this way when you are alone is good, and being silent in this way *together* is particularly dynamic and healing.

## the sound of no sound

Silence is often described as the absence of sound, yet it's also a very powerful sound. I remember the winter of 2013–2014 was not so cold in France, but we heard it was very cold in North America. There were more than the usual number of snowstorms, and sometimes the temperature went below minus 20 degrees Celsius. I saw a picture of Niagara Falls at about its coldest. The falls had stopped falling. The water *couldn't* fall anymore; it was frozen. I saw that image and was very impressed. The cascade of water had stopped—together with the sound.

About forty years ago I was in Chiang Mai, in the northeast of Thailand, in a retreat for young people. I was staying in a hut near a stony creek, and there was always the sound of water falling. I enjoyed breathing and washing my clothes and taking a nap on the big stones in the creek. Wherever I was, I heard that sound of water falling. Day and night, I heard the same sound. I looked at the bushes and trees around and thought, *Since their birth they have heard this sound. Suppose this sound stopped and for the first time they heard the no-sound—silence.* Just imagine that, if you can. Suddenly the water stops flowing, and all these plants that from their birth have always, day and night, heard that cascading sound hear it no longer. Think how surprised they would be to hear, for the first time in their lives, the sound of no sound.

## five true sounds

*Bodhisattva* is the Buddhist term for someone with great compassion whose life work is to ease people's suffering. Buddhism talks about a bodhisattva named Avalokiteshvara, the Bodhisattva of Deep Listening. The name Avalokiteshvara means "the one who listens deeply to the sounds of the world."

According to Buddhist tradition, Avalokiteshvara has the capacity to listen to all kinds of sounds. He can also utter five different kinds of sounds that can heal the world. If you can find silence within yourself, you can hear these five sounds.

The first is the Wonderful Sound, the sound of the wonders of life that are calling you. This is the sound of the birds, of the rain, and so on.

*God is a sound. The creator of the cosmos is a sound. Everything begins with the sound.*

The second sound is the Sound of the One Who Observes the World. This is the sound of listening, the sound of silence.

The third sound is the Brahma Sound. This is the transcendental sound, *om,* which has a long history in Indian spiritual thought. The tradition is that the sound *om* has the innate power to create the world. The story goes that the cosmos, the world, the universe was created by that sound. The Christian Gospel of John has the same idea: "In the beginning there was the word" (John 1:1). According to the Vedas, the oldest Hindu texts, that world-creating word is *om.* In Indian Vedic tradition, this sound is the ultimate reality, or God.

Many modern astronomers have come to believe something similar. They have been looking for the beginning of time, the beginning of the cosmos, and they hypothesize that the very beginning of the universe was "the big bang."

The fourth sound is the Sound of the Rising Tide. This sound symbolizes the voice of the Buddha. The teaching of the Buddha can clear away misunderstanding, remove affliction, and transform everything. It's penetrating and effective.

The fifth sound is the Sound That Transcends All Sounds of the World. This is the sound of impermanence, a reminder not to get caught up in or too attached to particular words or sounds. Many scholars have made the Buddha's teaching complicated and difficult to understand. But the Buddha said things very simply and did not get caught up in words. So if a teaching is too complicated, it's not the sound of the Buddha. If what you're hearing is too loud, too noisy, or convoluted, it's not the voice of the Buddha. Wherever you go, you can hear that fifth sound. Even if you're in prison, you can hear the Sound That Transcends All Sounds of the World.

## your deepest concern

When you've been able to still all the noise inside of you, when you've been able to establish silence, a thundering silence, in you, you begin to hear the deepest kind of calling from within yourself. Your heart is calling out to you. Your heart is trying to tell you something, but you haven't yet been able to hear it, because your mind has been full of noise. You've been pulled away all the time, day and night. You've been full of thoughts, especially negative thoughts.

In our daily lives many of us spend most of our time looking for comforts—material comforts and affective comforts—in order to merely survive. That takes all our time. These are what we might call the *daily concerns*. We are preoccupied with our daily concerns: how to have enough money, food, shelter, and other material things. We also have affective concerns: whether or not some particular person loves us, whether or not our job is secure. We worry all day because of those kinds of questions. We may be trying to find a relationship that is good enough to endure, one that is not too difficult. We're looking for something to rely on.

We may be spending 99.9 percent of our time worrying about these daily concerns—material comforts and affective concerns—and that is understandable, because we need to have our basic needs met to feel safe. But many of us worry far, far beyond having our needs met. We are physically safe, our hunger is satisfied, we have a roof over our heads, and we have a loving family; and still we can worry constantly.

The deepest concern in you, as in many of us, is one you may not have perceived, one you may not have heard. Every one of us has an *ultimate concern* that has nothing to do with material or affective concerns. What do we want to do with our life? That is the question. We are here, but *why* are we here? Who are we, each of us individually? What do we want to do with our life? These are questions that we don't typically have (or make) the time to answer.

These are not just philosophical questions. If we're not able to answer them, then we don't have peace—and we don't have joy, because no joy is possible without some peace. Many of us feel we can never answer these questions. But with mindfulness, you can hear their response yourself, when you have some silence within. You can find some answers to these questions and hear the deepest call of your heart.

When you ask the question, "Who am I?"—if you have enough time and concentration—you may find some surprising answers. You may see that you are a continuation of your ancestors. Your parents and your ancestors are fully present in every cell of your body; you are their continuation. You don't have a separate self. If you remove your ancestors and your parents from you, there's no "you" left.

You may see that you're made of elements, like water for example. If you remove the water from you, there's no "you" left. You're made of earth. If you remove the element earth from you, there's no "you" left. You're made of air. You need air desperately; without air you cannot survive. So if you remove the element of air from you, there's no "you" left. And there's the fire element, the element of heat, the element of light, in you. You know that you are made of light. Without sunlight, nothing can grow on Earth. If you continue to look, you see that you are made of the sun, one of the biggest stars in the galaxy. And you know that the Earth, as well as yourself, is made of the stars. So you are the stars. On a clear night, look up, and you can see that you are the stars above. You're not just the tiny body you normally may think of as "yourself."

## no need to run

Mindfulness gives you the inner space and quietness that allow you to look deeply, to find out who you are and what you want to do with your life. You won't feel the need to make yourself run after meaningless pursuits anymore. You've been running, looking for something, because you think that thing is crucial for your peace and happiness. You push yourself to achieve this and that condition so that you can be happy. You believe you don't have enough conditions to be happy right now, and so you develop the habit many people have, of constantly running after one thing or another. "I cannot be peaceful now, I cannot stop and enjoy things now, because I need more conditions before I can be happy." You actually stifle the natural joie de vivre that is your birthright. But life is full of wonders, including wondrous sounds. If you can *be* here, if you can be free, then you can be happy right here and right now. You don't have to run anymore.

*The practice of mindfulness*

*is very simple.*

———————

You stop, you breathe, and you still your mind.

*You come home to yourself so*

*that you can enjoy the here and*

*now in every moment.*

———————

All the wonders of life are already here. They're calling you. If you can listen to them, you will be able to stop running. What you need, what we *all* need, is silence. Stop the noise in your mind in order for the wondrous sounds of life to be heard. Then you can begin to live your life authentically and deeply.

## one

# a steady diet of noise

Unless you live alone in the mountains without electricity, chances are you're absorbing a constant stream of noise and information all day long, without interruption. Even if no one is speaking to you and you're not listening to the radio or some other sound system, there are billboards, telephone calls, text messages, social media, computer screens, bills, flyers, and many other ways that words and sounds reach us. It sometimes can be impossible to find a corner of an airport boarding area without a television blaring. Many people's morning commute is spent absorbing tweets, texts, news, games, and updates on their phones.

Even in those rare moments when there is no sound, text, or other information coming in from outside, our heads are filled with a constant loop of thoughts. How many minutes each day, if any, do you spend in true quiet?

*Silence is essential. We need silence,*

*just as much as we need air,*

*just as much as plants need light.*

*If our minds are crowded with*

*words and thoughts, there is*

*no space for us.*

———

People who live in an urban setting get used to a certain level of ambient noise. There's always someone shouting, traffic honking, or music blaring. The constancy of perpetual noise can actually become reassuring. I know friends who go to the countryside for a weekend, or who go to a meditation retreat, and find the silence scary and unsettling. The silence doesn't feel safe or comfortable because they are used to a background of constant noise.

Plants can't grow without light; people can't breathe without air. Everything that lives needs space to grow and to become.

## fear of silence

I have the impression that many of us are afraid of silence. We're always taking in something—text, music, radio, television, or thoughts—to occupy the space. If quiet and space are so important for our happiness, why don't we make more room for them in our lives?

One of my longtime students has a partner who is very kind, a good listener, and not overly talkative; but at home her partner always needs to have the radio or TV on, and he likes a newspaper in front of him while he sits and eats his breakfast.

I know a woman whose daughter loved to go to sitting meditation at the local Zen temple and encouraged her to give it a try. The daughter told her, "It's really easy, Mom. You don't have to sit on the floor;

there are chairs available. You don't have to do anything at all. We just sit quietly." Very truthfully the woman replied, "I think I'm afraid to do that."

We can feel lonely even when we're surrounded by many people. We are lonely together. There is a vacuum inside us. We don't feel comfortable with that vacuum, so we try to fill it up or make it go away. Technology supplies us with many devices that allow us to "stay connected." These days, we are *always* "connected," but we continue to feel lonely. We check incoming e-mail and social media sites multiple times a day. We e-mail or post one message after another. We want to share; we want to receive. We busy ourselves all day long in an effort to connect.

What are we so afraid of? We may feel an inner void, a sense of isolation, of sorrow, of restlessness. We may feel desolate and unloved. We may feel that we lack something important. Some of these feelings are very old and have been with us always, underneath all our doing and our thinking. Having plenty of stimuli makes it easy for us to distract ourselves from what we're feeling. But when there is silence, all these things present themselves clearly.

## a  s m o r g a s b o r d   o f   s t i m u l i

All the sounds around us and all the thoughts that we're constantly replaying in our minds can be thought of as a kind of food. We're familiar with edible food, the kind of food we physically chew and swallow. But that's not the only kind of food we humans consume; it's just one kind. What we read, our conversations, the shows we watch, the online games we play, and our worries, thoughts, and anxieties are all food. No wonder we often don't have space in our consciousness for beauty and silence: we are constantly filling up on so many other kinds of food.

There are four kinds of food that every person consumes every day. In Buddhism, we call these kinds of food the Four Nutriments. They are edible food; sense impressions; volition; and consciousness, both individual and collective.

The edible food is, of course, the food that you eat with your mouth every day. The second food, sense impressions, is the sensory experiences you receive through your eyes, ears, nose, tongue, body, and mind. This includes what you hear, what you read, what you smell, and what you touch. It includes your phone and text messages, the sound of the bus outside your window, and the billboard you read as you pass by it. Although these things are not edible food, they are information and ideas that come into your consciousness and you consume them every day.

The third source of nutriment is volition. Volition is your will, your concern, your desire. This is food because it "feeds" your decisions, your actions, and your movements. Without any volition, without any desire to do anything, you wouldn't move; you would simply wither.

The fourth kind of food is consciousness. This food includes your individual consciousness and the way your mind feeds itself and feeds your thoughts and actions. It also includes collective consciousness and how it affects you.

All of these foods can be healthy or unhealthy, nourishing or toxic, depending on what we consume, how much we consume, and how aware we are of our consumption. For example, we sometimes eat junk food that makes us sick, or drink too much when we're upset about something, in the hopes of distracting ourselves even if afterward that consumption makes us feel worse.

We do the same thing with the other nutriments. With sensory food, we may have the awareness to take in media that are wholesome and enlightening, or on the other hand we may use video games, movies, magazines, or even engaging in gossip in order to distract ourselves from our suffering. Volition can also be healthy (constructive motivation) or unhealthy (craving and obsession). Likewise, collective consciousness can be healthy or unhealthy. Think of how affected you are by the mood or the consciousness of the group you are in, whether that group is supportive, happy, angry, gossipy, competitive, or listless.

Because each nutriment affects us so deeply, it's important to be aware of what and how much we are consuming. Our awareness is the key to our protection. Without protection, we absorb far too many toxins. Without realizing it, we become full of toxic sounds and toxic consciousness that make us ill. Mindful awareness is like a sunscreen protecting the sensitive skin of a newborn baby. Without it, the skin would blister and burn. With the protection of our mindfulness, we are able to stay healthy and safe and take in only those nutriments that help us thrive.

## ֹ edible food

Most of us are aware that what we eat affects how we feel. Junk foods can make us feel tired, crabby, jittery, guilty, and often only momentarily satisfied. Fruits and vegetables, on the other hand, make us feel energetic, healthy, and well-nourished. Often we eat something not because we're hungry, but to console ourselves or to distract ourselves from uncomfortable feelings. Suppose you feel worried or lonely. You don't like this feeling, so you open the refrigerator and look for something to eat. You know that you aren't hungry, that you don't *need* to eat. You find something to eat anyway, because you want to cover up the feeling inside.

When we have a retreat at any of our practice centers, we offer three healthy vegetarian meals every day, lovingly prepared with mindfulness. Still, there are participants who are worried about food. I have a friend who, when he first came to a mindfulness retreat, could think only about when he was next going to eat. For the first two days of the retreat, he was hungry all the time, and he didn't like the fact that there were lines for meals. He worried that the food would run out, even though it never did. Usually, he would leave whatever activity he was doing early so he could be one of the first in line for meals.

On the third day of the retreat, this friend was in a sharing group where he was able to talk about some of his feelings about his father (who had recently died), and he got a lot of support from the group. The group ran a little late, but when he got to the meal line, he realized he wasn't anxious. He had a feeling there would be enough food and he would be okay. I'm very glad we didn't run out of rice and vegetables that particular day!

## sense impressions

Sensory food is what we take in with our senses and our mind—everything we see, smell, touch, taste, and hear. External noise falls into this category, such as conversations, entertainment, and music. What we read and the information we absorb is also sensory food.

Perhaps even more than edible food, the sensory

food we consume affects how we feel. We may pick up a magazine or go on the Internet, looking at pictures and listening to music. We want to connect and be informed. We want to enjoy ourselves. These are fine reasons to consume sensory food, but often our *real* purpose in those moments is simply to run away from ourselves and cover up the suffering inside. When we listen to music, read a book, or pick up a newspaper, it's usually not because we truly need that activity or information. We often do it mechanically—perhaps because we're used to doing it, or we want to "kill time" and fill up the discomfiting sense of empty space. We may do it to avoid encountering ourselves. Many of us are afraid of going home to ourselves because we don't know how to handle the suffering inside us. That's why we're always reaching for more and more sense impressions to consume.

*We are what we feel and perceive.*

*If we are angry, we are the anger.*

*If we are in love, we are the love.*

*If we look at a snowy mountain*

*peak, we are the mountain. While*

*dreaming, we are the dream.*

———

A teenager recently confessed to me that he spends at least eight hours a day playing video games. He can't stop. In the beginning he took to games in order to forget that he wasn't feeling good about life, that he didn't feel understood in his family, school, and community. Now he's addicted to them. He thinks about video games all the time, even in the moments he isn't playing them. Many of us can relate to some version of this, trying to fill up the loneliness and emptiness inside us with sense impressions.

Our senses are our windows to the outside world. Many of us leave our windows open all the time, allowing the sights and sounds of the world to invade us, penetrate us, and compound the suffering in our sad, troubled selves. We feel terribly cold and lonely and afraid. Do you ever find yourself watching an awful

TV program, unable to turn it off? The raucous noises and explosions of gunfire are upsetting, yet you don't get up and turn it off. Why do you torture yourself in this way? Don't you want to give yourself some relief and close your sense windows? Are you afraid of solitude, of the emptiness and the loneliness you may find when you face yourself alone?

Watching a bad TV program, we are the TV program. We can be anything we want, even without a magic wand. So why do we open our windows to bad movies and TV programs—movies made by sensationalist producers in search of easy money, movies that make our hearts pound, our fists tighten, and that send us back into the streets exhausted?

Conversation is also sensory food. Suppose you talk to a person who is full of bitterness, envy, or craving. During the conversation, you take in that person's energy of despair. In truth, much of the sensory food we consume makes us feel worse instead of better. We find ourselves thinking more and more that we are not enough, that we need to buy something or change something in ourselves to make ourselves better.

But we can always make the choice to protect our peace. That doesn't mean shutting all our windows all of the time, for there are many miracles in the world we call "outside." Open your windows to these miracles. But look at any one of them with the light of awareness. Even while sitting beside a clear, flowing stream, listening to beautiful music, or watching an excellent movie, don't entrust yourself entirely to the stream, the music, or the film. Continue to be aware of yourself and your breathing. With the sun of awareness shining in you, you can avoid most dangers—and you will experience the stream being purer, the music more harmonious, and the soul of the artist completely visible in the film.

## volition

Volition, our primary intention and motivation, is the third kind of nutriment. It feeds us and gives us purpose. So much of the noise around us, whether advertisements, movies, games, music, or conversation, gives us messages about what we should be doing, what we should look like, what success looks like, and who we should be. Because of all this noise, it's rare that we pay attention to our true desire. We act, but we don't have the space or quiet to act *with intention.*

If we don't have any purpose feeding us, we are just drifting. There are certain people whom I see only once a year. When I ask them what they have done in the past year, many can't remember. Sometimes, for most of us, days, whole weeks, and even months go by like this, in a fog. This is because we're not aware of our intention on those days. Sometimes, it seems the only intention in us is just to make it through the day.

Whenever we act, whether to walk to the store, call a friend, take a step, or go to work, we have an intention, a motivation that gets us moving, whether we realize it or not. Time goes by very quickly; one day we may be surprised to discover our life is nearing its end, and we don't know what we've done with all the time we've lived. Maybe we've wasted entire days in anger, fear, and jealousy. We rarely offer ourselves the time and space to consider: *Am I doing what I most want to be doing with my life? Do I even know what that is?* The noise in our heads and all around us drowns out the "still, small voice" inside. We are so busy doing "something" that we rarely take a moment to look deeply and check in with our deepest desires.

Volition is a tremendous source of energy. But not all volition comes from the heart. If your volition is only to make enormous amounts of money or to have the biggest number of Twitter followers, that may not lead you to a satisfying life. Many people who have a lot of money and power are not happy; they feel quite lonely. They don't have time to live their lives authentically. Nobody understands them, and they don't understand anyone.

*To fully experience this life as*

*a human being, we all need to*

*connect with our desire to realize*

*something larger than our individual*

*selves. This can be motivation enough*

*to change our ways so we can*

*find relief from the noise that*

*fills our heads.*

———

You can spend your whole life listening to internal and external messages without ever hearing the voice of your deepest desire. You don't have to be a monk or a martyr to do this. If you have space and silence to listen deeply to yourself, you may find within you a strong desire to help other people, to bring love and compassion to others, to create positive transformation in the world. Whatever your job—whether you lead a corporation, serve food, teach, or take care of others—if you have a strong and clear understanding of your purpose and how your work relates to it, this can be a powerful source of joy in your life.

## individual consciousness

Even if we go on a sensory fast, cutting off outside noises and input, we are still consuming a potent source of food: our own consciousness. This, along with collective consciousness, is the fourth source of food.

When we direct our attention to certain elements of our consciousness, we're "consuming" them. As with our meals, what we consume from our consciousness may be wholesome and healthy, or it may be toxic. For example, when we're having a cruel or angry thought and we replay it over and over again in our mind, we are consuming toxic consciousness. If we are noticing the beauty of the day or feeling grateful for our health and the love of those around us, we are consuming healthy consciousness.

Every one of us has the capacity to love, to forgive, to understand, and to be compassionate. If you know how to cultivate these elements within your consciousness, your consciousness can nourish you with this healthy kind of food that makes you feel wonderful and benefits everyone around you. At the same time, in everyone's consciousness there is also the capacity for obsession, worry, despair, loneliness, and self-pity. If you consume sensory food in a way that nourishes these negative elements in your consciousness—if you read tabloids, play violent electronic games, spend time online envying what others have done, or engage in a mean-spirited conversation—the anger, despair, or jealousy becomes a stronger energy in your consciousness. You are cultivating the kind of food in your own mind that isn't healthy for you. Even after you have walked away from the book or the computer game, your mind may continue to revisit and re-consume those toxic elements for hours, days, or weeks afterward, because they have watered the negative seeds in your consciousness.

There are plants that can make you sick, such as hemlock and belladonna. If you consume them, you suffer. People usually don't deliberately grow these plants in their garden. Similarly, you can choose to cultivate the healthy things in your consciousness that will nourish you rather than the toxic things that will poison you and make you suffer.

Whether we're conscious of it or not, we are continually watering one thing or another in our mind—things that we almost certainly will consume again later on. What we water and consume unconsciously may show itself to us in our dreams. It may manifest as something we blurt out in a conversation, and then we wonder, "Where in the world did *that* come from?!" We can do a lot of damage to ourselves and to our relationships when we don't pay attention to what we're taking into ourselves and cultivating in our mind.

## collective consciousness

In addition to our individual consciousness, we also take in the collective consciousness. Just as the Internet is made up of many individual sites, collective consciousness is made up of individual consciousnesses. And each individual consciousness contains all the elements of the collective consciousness. The collective consciousness can be destructive, such as the violence of an angry mob or, more subtly, the hostility of a group of people who are judgmental or gossipy. On the other hand, like individual consciousness, collective consciousness can be healing—for example, when you're with loving friends or family, or with strangers in a situation of mutual appreciation such as listening to music, seeing art, or being in nature. When we surround ourselves with people who are committed to understanding and loving, we're nourished by their presence and our own seeds of understanding and love are watered. When we surround ourselves with people who gossip, complain, and are constantly critical, we absorb these toxins.

I had a musician friend who immigrated to California as a young man and then, when he grew old, moved back to Vietnam. People asked the old man why he had returned. "In California you could eat whatever you wanted, do anything you liked, and the hospitals were excellent," they pointed out. "You could buy whatever instruments you wanted; you had everything. Why did you come back to Vietnam?" He answered that in California he was surrounded by expatriates who were full of hatred and anger, and every time they visited him, they poisoned him with their resentment. He didn't want to absorb all that rage and bitterness in the precious few years he had left in this life. So he sought a place where he could live surrounded by a happier, more caring community.

If we live in a neighborhood that is full of violence, fear, anger, and despair, we consume the collective energy of anger and fear even if we don't want to. If we live in a neighborhood that is very loud, with horns blaring and alarms sounding, we consume that energy and anxiety. Unless circumstances beyond our control oblige us to live in such a neighborhood, we can instead choose surroundings that are quiet and supportive. And even within noisy surroundings, we can create an oasis of silence. We can be positive agents of change.

If you are beginning to think about how to bring more silence and space into your life so that you can cultivate joy, remember that none of us can do this alone. It's much easier to achieve and appreciate quiet when you have a supportive environment. If you can't bring yourself into a quieter, more peaceful physical environment, surround yourself as much as you can with people who help foster a collective energy of calm and compassion. Consciously choosing what and who you surround yourself with is among the keys to finding more space for joy.

# practice:
# nourishing

When feeling lonely or anxious, most of us have the habit of looking for distractions, which often leads to some form of unwholesome consumption—whether eating a snack in the absence of hunger, mindlessly surfing the Internet, going on a drive, or reading. Conscious breathing is a good way to nourish body and mind with mindfulness. After a mindful breath or two, you may have less desire to fill yourself up or distract yourself. Your body and mind come back together and both are nourished by your mindfulness of breathing. Your breath will naturally grow more relaxed and help the tension in your body to be released.

Coming back to conscious breathing will give you a nourishing break. It will also make your mindfulness stronger, so when you want to look into your anxiety or other emotions you'll have the calm and concentration to be able to do so.

Guided meditation has been practiced since the time of the Buddha. You can practice the following exercise when you sit or walk. In sitting meditation, it's important for you to be comfortable and for your spine to be straight and relaxed. You can sit on a cushion with your legs crossed or on a chair with your feet flat on the floor. With the first in-breath, say the first line of the meditation below silently to yourself, and with the out-breath say the second line. With the following in- and out-breaths, you can use just the key words.

*Breathing in, I know I'm breathing in.*
*Breathing out, I know I'm breathing out.*
*(In. Out.)*

*Breathing in, my breath grows deep.*
*Breathing out, my breath grows slow.*
*(Deep. Slow.)*

*Breathing in, I'm aware of my body.*
*Breathing out, I calm my body.*
*(Aware of body. Calming.)*

*Breathing in, I smile.*
*Breathing out, I release.*
*(Smile. Release.)*

*Breathing in, I dwell in the present moment.*
*Breathing out, I enjoy the present moment.*
*(Present moment. Enjoy.)*

# two

# radio non-stop thinking

Even if we are not talking with others, reading, listening to the radio, watching television, or interacting online, most of us don't feel settled or quiet. This is because we're still tuned to an *internal* radio station, Radio NST (Non-Stop Thinking).

Even when we're sitting still, with no external stimuli, an endless internal dialogue may be going on in our head. We're constantly consuming our thoughts. Cows, goats, and buffalo chew their food, swallow it, then regurgitate and rechew it multiple times. We may not be cows or buffalo, but we ruminate just the same on our thoughts—unfortunately, primarily negative thoughts. We eat them, and then we bring them up to chew again and again, like a cow chewing its cud.

We need to learn to turn off Radio NST. It's not good for our health to consume from our own consciousness this way. In Plum Village, the retreat center in France where I live, we focus on practicing mindful consumption of sensory food as well as edible food. Not only do we choose not to drink alcohol or eat meat, we also do our best to talk and to think as little as possible while we are eating, drinking, washing dishes, or doing any other activity. This is because while walking, for example, if we are talking or thinking at the same time, we get caught up in the conversation or thoughts we're having and get lost in the past or the future, our worries or our projects. People can easily spend their entire lives doing just that. What a tragic waste! Let us instead really *live* these moments that are given to us. In order to be able to live our life, we have to stop that radio inside, turn off our internal discourse.

How can we enjoy our steps if our attention is given over to all that mental chatter? It's important to become aware of what we *feel*, not just what we think. When we touch the ground with our foot, we should be able to feel our foot making contact with the ground. When we do this, we can feel a lot of joy in just being able to walk. When we walk, we can invest all our body and mind into our steps and be fully concentrated in each precious moment of life.

In focusing on that contact with the earth, we stop being dragged around by our thoughts and begin to experience our body and our environment in a wholly different way. Our body is a wonder! Its functioning is the result of millions of processes. We can fully appreciate this only if we stop our constant thinking and have enough mindfulness and concentration to be in touch with the wonders of our body, the Earth, and the sky.

It's not that thinking is necessarily always bad. Thinking can be very productive. Thoughts are often the product of our feelings and our perceptions. So thinking may be seen as a kind of fruit. Some kinds of fruit are nourishing. Others are not. If we have a lot of worry, fear, or anguish, that is very fertile ground for thinking that is completely useless, nonproductive, and harmful.

We are our thoughts; but we are at the same time much more than *just* our thoughts. We are also our feelings, our perceptions, our wisdom, our happiness, and our love. When we know we are more than our thoughts, we can make the determination not to allow our thinking to take over and dominate us. Do our thoughts support our true intention in life? If not, we need to push the "reset" button. If we aren't aware of our thoughts, they run rampant through our mind and take up residence there. They don't wait for an invitation.

## the habit of
## negative thinking

Buddhist psychology identifies at least two major parts of our mind. Store consciousness is the lower part of our mind. This is where all the seeds of the thoughts and emotions we have inside us are stored. There are all kinds of seeds: seeds of love, faith, forgiveness, joy, and happiness, and also seeds of suffering, like anger, enmity, hatred, discrimination, fear, agitation, and so on. All the talents as well as the weaknesses of our ancestors have been transmitted to us through our parents, and they dwell in the depths of our consciousness in the form of seeds.

Store consciousness is like the basement of a house, while mind consciousness, the upper part of the mind, is like the living room. The seeds are stored in the basement, and whenever one is stimulated—or, as we often say, "watered"—it comes up and manifests on the level of mind consciousness. Then it's no longer a dormant seed but is a zone of energy called a mental formation. If it's a wholesome seed like mindfulness or compassion, we enjoy its company. But when an unwholesome seed is stimulated, it can take over our living room like an unwelcome guest.

For example, while we're watching television, perhaps the seed of craving in us is touched, and then it comes up to manifest on the level of mind consciousness as the energy of craving. Another example: when the seed of anger lies dormant in us, we feel happy; we feel joyful. But when somebody comes along and says or does something that waters that seed of anger, it will manifest on the level of mind consciousness as an energy zone of anger.

We practice to touch and water the wholesome seeds so that they can manifest in our daily life, and we practice *not* to water the seeds of hatred or craving. In Buddhism this is called the practice of diligence. In Plum Village, we call it selective watering. For example, when the seeds of violence and hatred lie still and quiet in our store consciousness, we feel a sense of well-being. But if we don't know how to take care of our consciousness, these seeds won't remain dormant, but will be watered and will manifest. It's important to be aware when an unwholesome seed manifests in mind consciousness and not to leave it there on its own. Whenever you see an unpleasant mental formation manifesting, call on the seed of mindfulness to manifest as a second energy in your mind consciousness in order to recognize, embrace, and calm the negative mental formation, so you can look deeply into the negativity to see its source.

Most of us have real anger and suffering living inside us. Perhaps in the past we were oppressed or mistreated, and all that pain is still right there, buried in our store consciousness. We haven't processed and transformed our relationship with what happened to us and we sit there alone with all that anger, hatred, despair, and suffering. If we were abused when we were young, every time our thinking mind goes back over that event, it's like we're experiencing the abuse all over again. We offer ourselves up to be abused over and over like that many times every day. That's ruminating on the toxic food of our consciousness.

During our childhood, we probably also had many happy moments. Nevertheless, we keep going back again and again to wallow in despair and other mental states that aren't healthy for us. It helps if we live in a good environment where our friends can remind us, "Dear friend, please don't ruminate." People used to say, "A penny for your thoughts." We can ask, "What are you ruminating on? Old suffering?" We can help each other to break out of our habitual negative thinking and get back in touch with the wonders that are right there inside us and around us. We can help each other not fall back into resurrecting the ghosts of suffering and despair that belong to the past.

## our thoughts in the world

Often our thinking goes around and around in circles, so we lose all our joy in living. The majority of our thinking not only doesn't help us; it actually can do harm. We might believe that we aren't causing any harm if we're just thinking something, but the reality is that the thoughts going through our mind also go out into the world. Just as a candle radiates light, heat, and scent, our thinking manifests itself in various ways, including in our speech and our actions.

*We are continued by our views*

*and by our thinking. Those are the*

*children we give birth to in*

*every moment.*

———————

When someone around us is feeling bad or is carried away by negative thinking, we can sense it. Every time we have a thought—whether about ourselves or the world, the past or the future—we somehow emit the thoughts and views that are at the base of that thinking. We produce thought, and our thought carries our views and the energy of our feelings.

When we get caught in negative thoughts and worries, it's easy to create misunderstanding and anxiety. When we stop the thinking and calm our mind, we create more space and openness.

So each of us has a choice. *You* have a choice. Your thoughts can make you and the world around you suffer more or suffer less. If you want to create a more collegial, harmonious atmosphere in your workplace or community, don't start by trying to change other people. Your first priority should be to find your own quiet space inside so you can learn more about yourself. This includes getting to know and understand your own suffering. When your practice is solid and you've already harvested some of the sweet fruits of getting to know yourself, you can consider ways you can make more room to bring silence, deep looking, understanding, and compassion into your work or community.

## mindfulness means reclaiming attention

Nonthinking is an art, and like any art, it requires patience and practice. Reclaiming your attention and bringing your mind and body back together for even just ten breaths can be very difficult at first. But with continued practice, you can reclaim your ability to be present and learn just to *be*.

Finding a few minutes to sit quietly is the easiest way to start training yourself to let go of your habitual thinking. When you sit quietly, you can observe how your thoughts rush in, and you can practice not ruminating on them and instead let them just come and go as you focus on your breath and on the silence inside.

I know some people who don't like to sit still. It's just not how they relax; some even find it very painful. One woman I know decided she could never meditate because it just "didn't work." So I asked her to take a walk with me. I didn't call it "walking meditation," but we walked slowly and with awareness, enjoying the air, the feel of our feet on the ground, and just walking together. When we came back, her eyes were bright and she seemed refreshed and clear.

*If you can take just a few minutes for yourself to calm your body, your feelings, and your perceptions in this way, joy becomes possible. The joy of true quiet becomes a daily healing food.*

Walking is a wonderful way to clear the mind without *trying* to clear the mind. You don't say, "Now I am going to practice meditation!" or "Now I am going to not think!" You just walk, and while you're focusing on the walking, joy and awareness come naturally.

In order to really enjoy the steps you make while walking, allow your mind to completely let go of any worry or plan. You don't need to put in a lot of time and effort to prepare yourself to stop thinking. With one in-breath taken in mindfulness, you have already stopped. You breathe in, and you make a step. With that in-breath, you have two or three seconds to stop the mental machinery. If Radio Non-Stop Thinking is blaring, don't let that spinning energy of dispersion carry you off, like a tornado. For many of us it happens all the time: rather than living our life, we allow ourselves to be swept away repeatedly throughout the day, day after day. With the practice of mindfulness, you can stay grounded in the present moment, where life and all its wonders are real and available to you.

In the beginning, you may need a little more time, maybe ten or twenty seconds of mindful breathing, before you can let your thinking go. You can take one step with each in-breath and one step with each out-breath. If your attention wanders, gently bring it back to your breathing.

Ten or twenty seconds is not a lot of time. One nerve impulse, one action potential, needs only a millisecond. Giving yourself twenty seconds is giving yourself twenty thousand milliseconds to stop the runaway train of thought. If you want, you can give yourself even more time.

In that short amount of time you can experience the bliss, the joy, the happiness of stopping. During that time of stopping, your body is able to heal itself. Your mind also has the capacity to heal itself. There is nothing and no one to prevent you from continuing the joy you've produced with a second step, a second breath. Your steps and your breath are always there to help you heal yourself.

As you're walking, you may see your mind being pushed and pulled around by an old, ingrained habit energy of anger or craving. In fact, that kind of energy might *always* be pushing you, whatever you're doing— even during your sleep. Mindfulness can recognize this habit energy. Having recognized it, simply smile to it—and give it a nice bath of mindfulness, of warm and spacious silence. With this practice, you are capable of letting negative habit energy go. While walking, while lying down, while washing the dishes, while brushing your teeth, you can always practice offering yourself this wide and warm embrace of silence.

Silence doesn't just mean not talking. Most of the noise we experience is the busy chatter inside our own head. We think and we rethink, around and around in circles. That's why at the start of each meal, we should remind ourselves to eat only our food and not our thoughts. We practice giving all our attention to eating. There's no thinking; we just bring our awareness to the food and to the people around us.

This doesn't mean we shouldn't ever think, or that we should suppress our thoughts. It simply means that when we're walking, we give ourselves the gift of taking a break from our thinking by keeping our attention on our breathing and our steps. If we really do need to think about something, we can stop walking and think the matter through with all our attention.

Breathing and walking in mindfulness puts us in touch with the miracles of life all around us, and our compulsive thinking will dissipate very naturally. Happiness arises as we become more aware of the many wonders available to us. If there's a full moon high in the sky and we're busy thinking about something else, the moon disappears. But if we pay attention to the moon, our thinking stops naturally; there's no need to force or scold ourselves or to forbid ourselves from thinking.

*Not talking, by itself, already can bring a significant degree of peace. If we can also offer ourselves the deeper silence of not thinking, we can find, in that quiet, a wonderful lightness and freedom.*

Shifting our attention away from our thoughts to come back home to what's really happening in the present moment is a basic practice of mindfulness. We can do it anytime, anywhere, and find more pleasure in life. Whether we're cooking, working, brushing our teeth, washing our clothes, or eating, we can enjoy this refreshing silencing of our thoughts and our speech.

The true practice of mindfulness doesn't require

sitting meditation or observing the outer forms of practice. It entails looking deeply and finding internal quiet. If we can't do that, we can't take care of the energies of violence, fear, cowardice, and hatred in us.

When our mind is racing and noisy, outward calm is only a pretense. But when we can find space and calm inside, then without effort we radiate peace and joy. We are able to help others and create a more healing environment around us, without uttering a single word.

## the space to realize dreams

Sometimes we hitch ourselves to large but essentially empty dreams, maybe because we're so busy just getting through the day that we don't believe we can actually live according to our deepest, most genuine desires. But the truth is that right here in our daily life, every breath and every step can be a concrete part of making our true dreams happen. If instead we pursue the prefabricated dreams that people sell us, having convinced ourselves that this or that brass ring is as good as it gets, we sacrifice the precious time we've been given to live and to love for empty ambitions with no real meaning. We may sell our entire lives for those things.

Many people come to a sad realization about this on their deathbed or in their later years. They suddenly wonder what they have to show for all those decades of work and stress. They may have become "victims of their own success," meaning they had attained the wealth and fame they'd sought, but had never had time and space to enjoy their life, to connect with people they loved. They'd had to keep running every day just to hold on to the status they had achieved.

But no one ever becomes a victim of his or her own happiness. You may find that when you make it your priority to follow the path of happiness, you also become more successful in your work. It's often the case that when people are happier and more peaceful, the quality of their work improves. But you do have to decide what your deepest aspiration really is. There are those who want to practice mindfulness in order to become more successful in their business or career, not in order to become happier and help others. Many people have asked me, "Can we use the practice of mindfulness to make more money?"

If you truly practice mindfulness, it will never cause harm. If the practice doesn't bring about more compassion, then it's not right mindfulness. If you feel that your dreams aren't coming true, you might think that you need to do more, or to think and strategize more. In fact, what you might need is less—less noise coming to you from both inside and outside—so that you have the space for your heart's truest intention to germinate and flourish.

# practice:
# stopping and letting go

Stopping brings body and mind together, back to the here and now. Only by stopping can you realize calm and concentration, and encounter life. By sitting quietly, stopping the activities of body and mind, and being silent within, you become more solid and concentrated, and your mind becomes clearer. Then it's possible to be aware of what's happening inside and around you.

Begin by stopping the physical running around you do with your body. When your body is still, when you don't need to pay attention to any activity other than your breathing, it will be much easier for your mind to let go of its own habitual running, although this can take some time and some practice.

Once you've learned how to stop your mind when your body is also stopped, you'll be able to stop your mind even when your body is moving. Focusing on the way your breathing combines with the physical movements of your daily activities, you can live with awareness instead of in forgetfulness.

Just like everything else in the world, your thoughts are impermanent. If you don't grasp a thought, it arises, stays for a while, and then fades away. Clinging to thoughts and harboring desires for such things as wealth, fame, or sensual pleasures can bring about craving and attachment, leading you down dangerous paths and causing suffering to yourself and others. Recognizing thoughts and desires, allowing them to come and go, gives you space to nourish yourself as well as to get in touch with your deepest aspirations.

Feel free to create your own verses to add to the guided meditation below.

> *Breathing in, I'm aware of my thoughts.*
> *Breathing out, I'm aware of their impermanent nature.*
> *(Thoughts. Impermanence.)*

> *Breathing in, I'm aware of my desire for wealth.*
> *Breathing out, I'm aware that wealth is*
> *impermanent.*
> *(Aware of desire for wealth. Impermanence.)*

> *Breathing in, I know that craving wealth can bring*
> *suffering.*
> *Breathing out, I let go of craving.*
> *(Aware of craving. Letting go.)*

*Breathing in, I'm aware of my desire for sensual
   pleasures.*
*Breathing out, I know that sensual desire is
   impermanent in nature.*
*(Aware of sensual desire. Impermanence.)*

*Breathing in, I'm aware of the danger of craving
   sensual pleasures.*
*Breathing out, I let go of my craving for sensual
   pleasures.*
*(Aware of craving. Letting go.)*

*Breathing in, I contemplate letting go.*
*Breathing out, I experience the joy of letting go.*
*(Contemplating letting go. Joy.)*

# three

# thundering silence

Our need to be filled up with one thing or another all the time is the collective disease of human beings in our era. And the marketplace is always ready to sell us every kind of product to fill ourselves up. Advertisers continually scare us into avoiding the supposedly pathetic situation of living life without this or that item. But many of the things we consume, both as edible food and as sensory impressions, have toxins in them. Just as we might feel worse after eating a whole bag of chips, we often feel worse after we spend many hours on social media sites or playing video games. After we consume like that in an effort to block out or cover up unpleasant feelings, somehow we only end up feeling even more loneliness, anger, and despair.

We need to stop consuming sensory food as a response to the compulsive urge to avoid ourselves. But that doesn't mean we should force ourselves to stop using our phones or the Internet altogether. Just as we need edible food, we also need sensory food. But we can be much more conscious and intelligent about choosing the kind of sensory food we will take in and especially about knowing why we are choosing, at that moment, to consume it.

There are many people who check their e-mail several times a day, searching for something new, even though most of the times they check, they don't find anything. The surest way to give ourselves something really new—a feeling of being refreshed, of being happy, of being at ease—is by opening up the space within us for the practice of mindfulness.

## letting go

Many Zen masters have said that nonthinking is the key to mindfulness meditation. To meditate does not mean to sit still and think! When thinking takes over, you lose contact with your body and your larger awareness. We humans hold very tightly to our thoughts, our ideas, and our emotions. We believe that they are real and that to let go of them would be to give up our very identity.

If you're like most people, you probably have a notion that there's some as yet unrealized condition that has to be attained before you can be happy. Maybe it's a diploma, a job promotion, an income level, or a relationship status. But that notion may be the very thing that prevents you from being happy. To release that notion and make space for true happiness to manifest, you first have to experience the truth that entertaining your current idea is making you suffer. You may have entertained that idea for ten or twenty years without ever having understood that it was interfering with your natural capacity to be happy.

One night I dreamed that I was a university student, about twenty-one years old. I was sixty-something when I had this dream, but in my dream I was quite young. I'd just been accepted into a class taught by a very distinguished professor, the most sought-after professor in the university. Delighted to get to be his student, I went to the appropriate office and inquired where the class was to be held. As I posed my question, someone walked into the office who looked exactly like me. The color of his clothing, his face—*everything* was identical. I was very surprised. Was he me or was he not me? I asked the staff person if this young man had also been accepted into the class. She said, "No, no way. You yes, but him—no."

The class was being held on the top floor of the building that same morning. I moved quickly to make it there on time and then, halfway up the stairs, I wondered aloud, "What is the subject of this class anyway?" Someone nearby told me it was music. I was very surprised, because I wasn't a student of music at all.

When I got to the classroom door, I looked in and saw that there were more than a thousand students in the class, a real assembly. Through the exterior window, I saw outside a beautiful landscape of mountain peaks covered in snow, and the moon and constellations above. I was deeply moved by the beauty. But then, just before the professor was about to come in, I was told we had to make a presentation on music— and I was to be the first presenter. I felt completely lost; I didn't know anything about music.

I searched in my pockets, looking for anything to help me, and felt something metallic. I took it out. It was a small bell. I told myself, "This is music. This is a musical instrument. I can make a presentation about the bell—yes, I can do it." I readied myself, but just at the moment someone announced that the professor was coming in, I woke up. I regretted that so much; if the dream had continued for another two or three minutes, I would have been able to see him, that extraordinary professor who everyone adored.

After I woke up, I tried to remember the details of the dream and to understand its meaning. I came to the conclusion that the other young man I'd seen in the office was also me, but maybe he was still caught in attachment to some kinds of views, and that was why he wasn't free enough to be accepted; he was perhaps a former aspect of myself that I had left behind as I gained insight that helped me drop my attachment to views.

To let go implies to let go *of something*. The something that we're holding on to may simply be a creation of our mind, an illusory perception of something, and not the reality of the thing itself. Everything is an object of our mind and is colored by our perception. You get an idea, and before you realize it, you've become stuck in that idea. You may get scared because of that idea you're believing in. You might even get sick because of it. Perhaps that idea brings you a lot of unhappiness and worries, and you would like to be free. But it's not enough that you *want* to be free. You have to give yourself enough space and quiet to become free.

Sometimes we need to take a bit more time to look deeply into an idea or an emotion and discover its roots. It came from somewhere, after all; it was formed perhaps in our childhood or even before we were born. Once we recognize the roots of an emotion or idea, we can begin to let it go.

The first step is to stop the thinking; we need to come back to our breathing and calm our body and mind. This will bring more space and clarity so that we can name and recognize the idea, desire, or emotion that's troubling us, say hello to it, and give ourselves permission to release it.

## finding answers
## without thinking

This is not to say we never have the right to think. Recently a monastic sister said to me, "I have so many difficulties to deal with, and if you tell me not to think, how can I solve anything?" But only *right thinking* is truly useful. Right thinking brings good fruits. In general, 90 percent or more of our thoughts are not right thinking; they just take us around and around in circles and lead us nowhere. The more we think like that, the more dispersion and agitation we bring to our mind and our body. That kind of thinking won't solve any problem.

Right thinking requires mindfulness and concentration. Say there's a problem we need to solve. It will take us much longer to reach a good resolution if we apply wrong thinking to it. We need to give our mind consciousness a rest and allow store consciousness to look for a solution. We have to take our intellectual and emotional "hands off the wheel" and entrust this question, this challenge, to our store consciousness, just as when planting a seed we have to entrust it to the earth and sky. Our thinking mind, our mind consciousness, is not the soil; it is only the hand that plants the seeds and cultivates the soil by practicing mindfulness of each thing we are doing as we go about our day. Our store consciousness is the fertile soil that will help the seed to germinate.

After entrusting that seed to the soil of our store consciousness, we need to be patient. While we sleep, our store consciousness is working. While we walk, while we breathe, if we don't let our thinking interfere with the process, the store consciousness is working. Then one day the solution appears, because we didn't take refuge in the thinking mind; we took refuge in our store consciousness.

We need to train ourselves in the way of meditation so we can entrust our questions, our difficulties, to our store consciousness. We can have confidence in it; and we use our mindfulness and concentration to help water the seed and care for the soil. One, two, or a few days later, a solution sprouts up and we call that a moment of awakening, a moment of enlightenment.

## the essence of stillness

When we release our ideas, thoughts, and concepts, we make space for our true mind. Our true mind is silent of all words and all notions, and is so much vaster than limited mental constructs. Only when the ocean is calm and quiet can we see the moon reflected in it.

Silence is ultimately something that comes from the heart, not from any set of conditions outside us. Living from a place of silence doesn't mean never talking, never engaging or doing things; it simply means that we are not *disturbed* inside; there isn't constant internal chatter. If we're truly silent, then no matter what situation we find ourselves in, we can enjoy the sweet spaciousness of silence.

There are moments when we think we're being silent because all around us there's no sound, but unless we calm our mind, talking is still going on all the time inside our head. That's not true silence. The practice is learning how to find silence in the midst of all the activities we do.

Try to change your way of thinking and your way of looking.

Sitting down to eat your lunch may be an opportune time for you to offer yourself the sweetness of silence. Even though others may be speaking, you have the ability to disengage from habitual thinking and be very silent inside. You can be in a crowded space, yet still enjoy silence and even solitude.

*Realize that silence comes from*

*your heart and not from the*

*absence of talk.*

———

Just as inner silence does not require outer silence, solitude does not necessarily have to mean there is no one physically around you. You realize the deep meaning of being alone when you are established firmly in the here and now, and you are aware of what is happening in the present moment. You use your mindfulness to become aware of every feeling, every perception you have. You're aware of what's happening around you, but you also stay fully present within yourself; you don't lose yourself to the surrounding conditions. That is real solitude.

## joyful versus oppressive silence

Sometimes when we think of silence, we think of an enforced restriction, such as a dictatorship shutting down freedom of expression, or an elder lecturing that "children should be seen and not heard," or one member of a household forbidding others from talking about a sensitive topic. That kind of silence is oppressive and only makes a situation worse.

Some of us know this kind of strained silence in our own families. If parents fight, there is often a painful silence afterward, and the whole family suffers. If everyone is angry or anxious, keeping silent can feed into an increasing collective anxiety and anger. That tense, simmering kind of silence is very negative. We cannot bear that kind of silence for long. It kills us. But voluntary silence is altogether different. When we know how to sit together, breathe together, connect with the spaciousness that's always available inside of us, and generate the energy of peace and relaxation and joy, that collective energy of silence is very healing, very nourishing.

Suppose you sit outside and pay attention to the sunshine, the beautiful trees, the grass, and the little flowers that are springing up everywhere. If you relax on the grass and breathe quietly, you can hear the sound of the birds, the music of the wind playing in the trees. Even if you are in a city, you can hear the songs of the birds and the wind. If you know how to quiet your churning thoughts, you don't have to turn to mindless consumption in a futile attempt to escape from uncomfortable feelings. You can just hear a sound, and listen deeply, and enjoy that sound. There is peace and joy in your listening, and your silence is an empowered silence. That kind of silence is dynamic and constructive. It's not the kind of silence that re-presses you.

In Buddhism we call this kind of silence thundering silence. It's very eloquent, and full of energy. Often we have retreats where thousands of people practice mindful breathing in and out silently together. If you have been part of something like this, you know how powerful a freely shared silence can be.

Have you ever noticed how much children, even very young ones, can enjoy silence? There's something very relaxing about this. In Plum Village, children of all ages can eat together and walk together silently and with great joy. We don't watch TV or play electronic games in our retreat center. I have one young friend who kicked and screamed the whole way to Plum Village the first time he came. He was eight years old. He and his parents had driven down from Paris and he didn't want to get out of the car because he knew that when he did, he wouldn't have any television or video games for a week. But he survived just fine, and made friends, and on the last day he didn't want to leave. Now he and his parents come every year and he looks forward to it. He's turning sixteen this year.

## noble silence

Conscious, intentional quiet is noble silence. Sometimes people assume that silence has to be serious, but there's a lightness in noble silence. Noble silence is a kind of silence that can have just as much joy in it as a good laugh.

Noble silence gives us a chance to recognize how our habit energy manifests in the ways we react to people and situations around us. There are those of us who make the choice to practice one or two weeks of silence, even three months of silence or more. After that much time in silence, we are able to transform our ways of responding to any number of situations. This silence is called noble because it has the power to heal. When you practice noble silence, you aren't just refraining from talking; you're calming and quieting your thinking. You're turning off Radio NST.

It's possible to recognize noble silence in someone else just by the way they behave. Some people always appear to be silent, but they're not truly silent. They're just somewhere else; they're not really present and available to life, to themselves, or to you. Other people put out an attitude that speaks volumes even when their mouths are shut. Maybe you've had the experience of being with someone who isn't saying anything, but you still get the distinct impression that he or she is criticizing you. That isn't noble silence, because noble silence promotes understanding and compassion. So be aware that, even if you don't say anything in words, you may be reacting strongly inside and people looking at your face may be able to tell.

Breathing mindfully and becoming aware of your responses to people and events around you is a deep practice. Instead of reacting, instead of even thinking, you allow yourself just to *be*. You practice mindfulness to be with your breath, your steps, the trees, the flowers, the blue sky, and the sunshine.

dhisattva is described as being a different arm and hand of the Buddha, with each bodhisattva representing a different kind of action. The legend goes that in a former life, Medicine King was called "the bodhisattva that everyone is glad to see." From time to time we meet a person like that, someone whom everyone is glad to see. Whether such people are children or adults, their presence is so wonderful, fresh, and pleasant that everyone is happy to see them.

The bodhisattva Medicine King practiced devotion and love. Do we need to love in order to succeed in our practice of enlightenment? The answer is yes. The role of affection in the growth of a child is very important. And the role of affection in the growth of knowledge and understanding is also very important. The loving presence of a mother is crucial for the growth of a baby, and the loving presence of a teacher and fellow practitioners is very important for us to develop in our practice. We need love in order to grow and to go far.

Medicine King grew well in his spiritual life and attained freedom and insight. He no longer identified himself with just his body. He mastered a kind of concentration called "the concentration that allows one to manifest in all kinds of bodies." If he needed to become a child, he became a child. If he needed to be a woman, he manifested as a woman. If he needed to be a businessman, he could manifest as a businessman. He wasn't caught by the idea that the body he found himself in was his. That's why he could release his body very easily. Medicine King saw that there was great suffering, poverty, and cruelty around him. As an offering, he poured fragrant oil over himself, set himself alight, and allowed himself to be burned by fire. The body of the bodhisattva Medicine King took millions of years to burn; and during that time, education took place. His burning body was a silent reminder to all who saw it of what he was willing to sacrifice.

Perhaps you have heard of monks in Vietnam who immolated themselves during the war in the 1960s. That action had its root in this chapter of the Lotus Sutra. People who don't consider this body to be themselves sometimes choose to use this body in order to get a message across. When the Vietnamese monks set themselves on fire, they were trying to send a silent message, to send the strongest message they possibly could, because so far no one had listened to the cries for help of those who were suffering. These monks were trying to say, by acts rather than words, that there was suppression, discrimination, and suffering in Vietnam. They used their body as a torch in an effort to create awareness of that suffering.

If you're not free, if you consider that this body is you, if you think that when this body disintegrates you will no longer be, then you cannot perform such an action. It's only when you are free and able to see yourself in many forms, not just in this body, that you can have the courage and the wisdom to offer yourself as a living torch.

The first monk to immolate himself, in 1963, was named Thich Quang Duc. *Quang* means "broad." *Duc* means "virtue." I knew him personally. He was a very loving person. When I was a young monk I stayed in his temple in Saigon. At that time I was editor of a Buddhist magazine and I was doing studies of other spiritual traditions. His temple had a collection of magazines that I made use of in my research.

Thich Quang Duc wrote compassionate letters urging the president of (South) Vietnam to stop his persecution of the Buddhists. He was part of a larger movement of monastics and laypeople who were organizing nonviolent responses to the increasing bloodshed. One day Thich Quang Duc had himself driven in an old car to an intersection in Saigon. He got out of the car, poured gasoline over himself, sat down beautifully in the lotus position, and struck a match. Five hours later the image of him sitting engulfed in flames in the middle of the intersection was available everywhere in the world, and people learned about the suffering of the Vietnamese people. A month or two later, the regime was brought down by a military coup, ending that policy of religious discrimination and persecution.

I was in New York at Columbia University giving a course on Buddhist psychology when I learned of Thich Quang Duc's death in the *New York Times*. Many people asked the question: "Isn't that a violation of the precept concerning not killing?" I wrote Dr. Martin Luther King Jr. a letter sharing with him that this was not really a suicide. When you commit suicide, you are in despair; you don't want to live anymore. But Thich Quang Duc was not like that. He wanted to live. He wanted his friends and other living beings to live. He loved being alive. But he was free enough to offer his body in order to get the message across: "We are suffering and we need your help." Because of the great compassion in him, he was able to sit very still in the fire, in perfect concentration. I shared with Dr. King my understanding that when Jesus died on the cross, he made the choice to die for the benefit of others—not out of despair but out of the will to help. That is exactly what Thich Quang Duc wanted to do. He committed this action not out of despair but out of hope and love, using his body in order to bring change to a desperate situation.

This burning was a kind of offering. What Thich Quang Duc and Medicine King wanted to offer in the act of self-immolation was not just their body, but their strong determination to help other living beings. That extraordinary determination was the basis of their dramatic action that successfully delivered an unforgettable message and silently transmitted their insight far and wide.

I tell this story not because I think you should do something this drastic, but simply to illustrate the power of silent action. We all want to change certain things or convince someone of something. If you have some small matter at work or in a relationship that you want to change and you've tried talking about it without results, consider the strength that is possible in silent action.

# practice:
# healing

If your daily life is full of hurrying, noise, or confusion, it's easy to forget to be aware of the wholesome and supportive elements that are all around you, such as the fresh air, the sun, and the trees.

The following exercise can be practiced anywhere, at any time. You just need to be in a place where you're comfortable breathing, relaxing, and smiling. A light smile relaxes all the muscles in your face and brings ease to body and mind, so don't just *say* the word "smile," really *do* it. You can also create your own nourishing verses.

You can renew yourself by getting in touch with the healing elements around you. You can also bring up refreshing images from your store consciousness to nourish you. For example, when you're in the middle of a busy city, you can recall what it's like to be in the mountains or at the seaside.

> *Breathing in, I'm aware of the air.*
> *Breathing out, I enjoy breathing the air.*
> *(Aware of the air. Feeling joy.)*

*Breathing in, I'm aware of the sun.*
*Breathing out, I smile to the sun.*
*(Aware of sun. Smiling.)*

*Breathing in, I'm aware of the trees.*
*Breathing out, I smile to the trees.*
*(Aware of trees. Smiling.)*

*Breathing in, I'm aware of the children.*
*Breathing out, I smile to the children.*
*(Aware of children. Smiling.)*

*Breathing in, I'm aware of the countryside air.*
*Breathing out, I smile to the countryside air.*
*(Countryside air. Smiling.)*

When we eat, we're often rushed; sometimes we don't even take the time to sit down. If that's true of you, please offer yourself the opportunity to eat mindfully as a human being, not a running robot. Before you eat, take a few moments to sit down, feel your weight supported by the chair (or the ground), quiet your thinking, and contemplate the food and its sources. The earth, the sun, the rain, labor, and many supportive conditions have come together so that your food could be brought to you. Be aware of how fortunate you are to have food to eat when so many people are hungry.

When you sit down to enjoy a meal with others, bring your awareness to the food and the people you are with. This can be a very joyful occasion of true community.

> *Breathing in, I'm aware of the food on my plate.*
> *Breathing out, I'm fortunate to have food to eat.*
> *(Aware of food. Feeling grateful.)*

> *Breathing in, I'm aware of the fields.*
> *Breathing out, I smile to the fields.*
> *(Aware of the fields. Smiling.)*

> *Breathing in, I'm aware of the many conditions that*
>     *brought this food to me.*
> *Breathing out, I feel grateful.*
> *(Aware of conditions. Feeling grateful.)*

> *Breathing in, I'm aware of those who are eating*
>     *together with me.*
> *Breathing out, I am grateful for their presence.*
> *(Eating together. Feeling grateful.)*

# four

## deep listening

M ost of the time, our head is so full of thoughts that we have no space to listen to ourselves or anyone else. We may have learned from our parents or in school that we have to remember lots of things, we have to retain a lot of words, notions, and concepts; and we think that this mental stockpile is useful for our life. But then when we try to have a genuine conversation with someone, we find it difficult to hear and understand the other person. Silence allows for deep listening and mindful response, the keys to full and honest communication.

Many couples who have been together for a long time come to mindfulness practice because they can't hear each other anymore. Sometimes one of the partners will say to me, "It's no use. She doesn't listen." Or

"He won't ever change. Talking to him is like talking to a brick wall." But it may be that the complaining partner is the one who doesn't have the space to listen. Each of us wants our partner to understand us, yes—but we also need to have the ability to really understand them.

Many of us are simply overloaded. We just don't seem to have the space for really hearing and understanding others. We may need to think a lot in our jobs, eight or nine hours a day, without stopping. We hardly ever give attention to our breathing or anything else but our thinking during this time. We believe that if we want to succeed, we can't afford to do anything other than that.

## listening with ease

Recently I met a woman from Paris who asked me for some guidance on her work as a kinesiologist. She wanted to know how she could most effectively do her job as a health adviser, to bring the greatest benefit to her clients. "If you have lightness and spaciousness in your heart," I told her, "then your speech will carry deep insight, and that will bring true communication." I shared with her the following.

*In order to practice right speech,*

*we need to first take the time to look*

*deeply into ourselves and into whoever*

*is in front of us so that our words*

*will be able to create mutual*

*understanding and relieve the*

*suffering on both sides.*

———

When we speak, of course we are only saying what we think is correct; but sometimes, because of the way we say it, the listener can't take it in, so our words don't have the desired effect of bringing more clarity and understanding to the situation. We need to ask ourselves, Am I speaking just to speak, or am I speaking because

I think these words can help someone heal? When our words are spoken with compassion, based on love and on our awareness of our interconnectedness, then our speech may be called right speech.

When we give an immediate reply to someone, usually we are just reeling off our knowledge or reacting out of emotion. When we hear the other person's question or comment, we don't take the time to listen deeply and look deeply into what has been shared; we just volley back a quick rejoinder. That's not helpful.

The next time someone asks you a question, don't answer right away. Receive the question or sharing and let it penetrate you, so that the speaker feels that he or she has really been listened to. All of us, but especially those whose profession is to help others, can benefit from training ourselves in this skill; we must practice in order to do it well. First and foremost, if we haven't listened deeply to ourselves, we can't listen deeply to others.

We need to cultivate a spiritual dimension of our life if we want to be light, free, and truly at ease. We need to practice in order to restore this kind of spaciousness. Only when we have been able to open space within ourselves, can we really help others. If I am out for a walk or on a public bus—anywhere, really—it is

very easy to notice if someone has a feeling of spaciousness. Perhaps you've met people like this—you don't
even know them well, but you feel comfortable with
them because they are easy and relaxed. They are not
already full of their own agenda.

If you open the space within yourself, you will
find that people, even someone who perhaps has been
avoiding you (your teenage daughter, your partner
with whom you were in a fight, your parent) will
want to come and be near you. You don't have to do
anything, or try to teach them anything, or even say
anything. If you are practicing on your own, creating
space and quiet within you, others will be drawn to
your spaciousness. People around will feel comfortable
just being around you because of the quality of your
presence.

This is the virtue of nonaction. We stop our thinking, bring our mind back to our body, and become
truly present. Nonaction is very important. It is not
the same thing as passivity or inertia; it's a dynamic
and creative state of openness. We just need to sit
there, very awake, very light; and when others come
sit with us, they feel at ease right away. Even though
we haven't "done" anything to help, the other person
receives a lot from us.

Having the space to listen with compassion is essential to being a true friend, a true colleague, a true parent, a true partner. A person doesn't need to be a mental health professional to listen well. In fact, many therapists *aren't* able to do it, because they are so full of suffering. They study psychology for many years and know a great deal about techniques, but in their heart they have suffering that they haven't been able to heal and transform, or they haven't been able to offer themselves enough joy and play to balance out all the pain they take in from clients, so they don't have the space to help very effectively. People pay these therapists a lot of money and go back to see them week after week hoping for healing; but counselors can't help if they haven't been able to listen to themselves with compassion. Therapists and counselors are human beings who suffer like everyone else. Their ability to listen to others is dependent first on their ability to listen compassionately to themselves.

If we want to help others, we need to have peace inside. This peace we can create with each step, each breath, and then we can help; otherwise, we are just wasting others' time—and taking their money if we're professionals. What all of us need first is ease, lightness, and peace in our own body and spirit. Only then can we truly listen to others.

This takes some practice. Take time each day to be with your breath and your steps, to bring your mind back to your body—to remember that you *have* a body! Take some time each day to listen with compassion to your inner child, to listen to the things inside that are clamoring to be heard. Then you will know how to listen to others.

## listening to the sound of a bell

Bells are used in many cultures around the world to help people come together, to create harmony within oneself and harmony with others. In many Asian countries, every family has at least one small bell in their home. You can use any kind of bell that makes a sound you enjoy. Use the sound of that bell as a reminder to breathe, to quiet your mind, to come home to your body, and to take care of yourself. In Buddhism, the sound of the bell is considered to be the voice of the

Buddha. Stop talking. Stop thinking. Come back to your breathing. Listen with all your being.

This way of listening allows peace and joy to penetrate every cell of your body. You listen not only with your ears, not only with your intellect; you invite all the cells in your body to join in listening to the bell.

A bell doesn't take up much space. You could surely find room on a table or a shelf somewhere, no matter where you live, even if you share a small room. Before you invite the bell to come home with you, you must make sure that the sound of the bell is good. The bell doesn't need to be big, but the sound should be pleasant.

Prepare yourself each time to listen and to receive the sound of the bell. Instead of "striking" the bell, "invite" the bell to sound. Look at the bell as a friend, an enlightened being that helps you wake up and come home to yourself. If you wish, you can set the bell on a small cushion—just like any other bodhisattva doing sitting meditation.

As you listen to the bell, practice breathing in and releasing all the tension that's built up, releasing the habit of your body, and especially your mind, to run. Although you may be sitting down, very often you are still running within. The bell is a welcome opportunity for you to go back to yourself, enjoy your in-breath and out-breath in such a way that you can release the tension and come to a *full* stop. The bell, and your response to it, helps stop the runaway train of thoughts and emotions racing through you all throughout the day and night.

In the morning, before you go to work or before the children go to school, everyone can sit down together and enjoy breathing for three sounds of the bell. That way you begin your day with peace and joy. It's nice to sit there, to breathe, either on your own or with your family, and look at a meaningful object in your home or a tree outside your window and smile. This can become a regular practice, a reliable refuge right there in your house or apartment. It doesn't take a long time, and it's richly rewarding. It is a very beautiful practice, the practice of peace, presence, and harmony in the home.

## breathing room

Dedicate a room or a portion of a room for meditation. This doesn't need to be a big space; if you have only a small corner of a room, that can work perfectly well, as long as you make it a quiet place reserved for peace and reflection. This is your breathing room, a small meditation hall. When a member of the household sits in that quiet place, others should not go in to try to talk to him or her. You have to agree with each other that this is a space reserved for peace and quiet.

I encourage you to sit down with all the members of your household and get everyone to agree that any time the atmosphere in the home is noisy, heavy, or tense, anyone has the right to go to the breathing room and invite the bell to sound. Everyone will practice breathing in and out, and endeavor to restore the calm, the peace, and the love they have lost sight of because of some unmindful, unskillful thought, word, or deed.

Any time someone has a problem, any time someone has a painful feeling or feels not peaceful, that person has the right to go to that space, sit down, invite the bell to sound, and breathe. And while somebody is doing that, the other people in the house have to respect it. If they are good practitioners, they will stop whatever they are doing, listen to the sound of the bell, and join the peaceful, mindful breathing. If they like, they can join that person in the breathing room.

So if your partner is not in a good mood, if your housemate has some worries, you may like to remind him or her, "Shall we go listen to the bell and breathe for a few minutes together?" That's something easy you can do. Or suppose your child gets angry about something. Then you hear the sound of the bell, and you know that your child is breathing. You pause from what you're doing and enjoy breathing in and out too. You support your child. And at bedtime it's nice if everyone sits down together to enjoy three sounds of the bell, nine times of breathing in and out.

People practicing breathing with a small bell in this way are able to enjoy much peace and harmony together. That is what I call true civilization. You don't need a lot of modern gadgets in order to be civilized. You need only a small bell, a quiet space, and your mindful in-breath and out-breath.


listening with our ancestors


People usually think that their ancestors have died, but that's not correct. Because we are here, alive, our ancestors continue to be alive in us. Our ancestors have transmitted themselves to us, with their talents, their experiences, their happiness, their suffering. They are fully present in every cell of our body. Our mother, our father, they are in us. We cannot take them out.

When we listen to the bell, we can invite all the cells in our body to join us in listening, and at the same time all the ancestors of all generations can join us in listening to the sound of the bell. If we know how to listen, peace can penetrate every cell of our body. And not only do we enjoy the peace, the relaxation, but all our ancestors in us get to enjoy the wonderful present moment. Perhaps, in their lives, they had a lot of suffering and didn't have many opportunities for joy. In you, they have this opportunity.

We generally think of listening as listening to those around us, but there are other kinds of listening. As was mentioned earlier, listening to ourselves is the first step in being able to listen well to others. What we find, if we listen within us, is no separate single voice, no separate self that simply appeared out of nowhere. This is one of the insights that come from practicing mindfulness. We discover how deeply connected we are with everyone who has come before us so that we may manifest. We are a community of cells, and all our ancestors are within us. We can hear their voices; we just need to listen.

## not caught in words

If we practice some time in silence each day, even if it's just a few minutes, we are much less prone to getting caught in words. Comfortable with practicing silence, we are free as a bird, in touch with the profound essence of things.

Vo Ngon Thong, one of the founders of Vietnamese Zen Buddhism, wrote, "Don't ask me anything more. My essence is wordless." To practice mindfulness of our speech, we have to be able to practice silence. Then we can examine carefully what our views are and what internal knots may be influencing our thinking. Silence is the best foundation for looking deeply. Confucius said, "The heavens do not say anything." Yet the heavens tell us so much if we know how to listen.

*If we listen from the mind of*

*silence, every birdsong and every*

*whispering of the pine branches*

*in the wind will speak to us.*

---

We all want to communicate with our loved ones, and there are many ways people communicate without words. Once we use words, we tend to turn them into labels that we think of as true. For example, words like "chores," "children," "listen," "man," and "woman" bring to mind certain images or assumptions, and it can be hard to see the full and evolving picture, beyond our mental constructs. If we truly want to communicate with our loved ones, we need to be aware of the nonverbal ways in which communication is taking place, whether consciously or unconsciously.

## a  f a s t  f o r  o u r  c o n s c i o u s n e s s

Many cultures practice fasting for a specific period of time for religious holidays, for initiation rituals, or for other reasons. Other people fast for health reasons. This is worth doing not only for our body but for our consciousness as well. Every day we take in a multitude of words, images, and sounds, and we need some time to stop ingesting all those things and let our mind rest. A day without the sensory food of e-mail, videos, books, and conversations is a chance to clear our mind and release the fear, anxiety, and suffering that can enter our consciousness and accumulate there.

Even if you don't think you can take a whole day without media, you can take a small break—a sound pause, if you will. Most people nowadays seem unable to live without a "sound track." As soon as they're alone (walking down the street, driving, sitting in a bus or train, or stepping out the door)—or even with their coworkers or their loved ones right in front of them—they try to fill up the tiniest bit of open mind space right away. If you decide to do just one solitary activity in true silence, whether it's being in the car, making breakfast, or walking around the block, you will be giving yourself a break from the constant stream of stimuli.

I know a person who found that the type of music played in her supermarket made her very sad. The songs reminded her of a difficult time in her life, and she saw herself focusing on the memories and not on her shopping. When she realized this, she made a conscious and intelligent choice to take good care of her consciousness. Now she puts in earplugs every time she goes to the supermarket, in order not to be distracted and depressed by the music.

You don't necessarily need to wear earplugs to have a sound fast. You can just take a few minutes each day that are deliberately quiet. Without words coming from outside or words swirling inside your mind, you have the chance to truly listen to yourself for a few minutes each day. This is a profound gift you can give to yourself that is also a gift to others, as it will help you listen more fully to them as well.

# practice:
# the four mantras

Practicing the Four Mantras is something anyone and everyone can do, even children. These mantras help you to cultivate deep listening and presence in your relationship with yourself and your loved ones. A mantra is a kind of magic formula that can transform a situation right away; you don't have to wait for results. What makes this practice effective is your mindfulness and concentration. Without these elements, it won't work.

To practice the mantras, it's crucial to quiet your thinking and to feel calm and spacious inside. Otherwise, you can't truly be there for the other person. Maintain that calm and spaciousness even when the other person responds. Especially when you practice the third and fourth mantras, if the other person has something to say, be sure to follow your breathing and listen silently and patiently, without judging or reacting. When you say the Four Mantras, you are using the silence inside, along with a few carefully chosen words, to bring healing, reconciliation, and mutual understanding. You are making space inside yourself and offering your spaciousness to the other person.

The first mantra is "Darling, I am here for you." When you love someone, you want to offer him or her the best you have, and that is your true presence. You can love only when you are *here,* when you are truly present. Simply saying the mantra doesn't make it so. You have to practice being here, by mindful breathing or mindful walking, or any other practice that helps you be present as a free person for yourself and for the person you love. Use this mantra with yourself first, to come back to yourself and create the silence and space inside that allow you to truly be present for the other person, and to authentically say the mantra.

The second mantra is "Darling, I know you are there, and I am very happy." To love means to ac-knowledge the presence of the person you love. This can be done only after you have prepared yourself to say the previous mantra: unless you are 100 percent *here,* you can't fully recognize another's presence, and that person may not feel truly loved by you.

When you are present and mindful, you are able to notice when the person you love suffers. In that moment, practice deeply to be fully present. Then go to him or to her and pronounce the third mantra: "Darling, I know you suffer; that's why I am here for you." When people suffer, they want the person they love to be aware of their suffering—that's very human and natural. If the person they love isn't aware of or ignores their suffering, they suffer much more. So use this mantra to communicate your awareness: it will be a great relief to the other person to know that you recognize his or her suffering. Even before you *do* anything to help, that person will suffer less already.

The fourth mantra, which you won't need often (but is powerful when you *do* need it), is "Darling, I suffer; please help." It is practiced when you yourself suffer, especially when you believe that your suffering has been caused by the other person. When that person is the one you love most, you suffer even more. So you go to that person, with your full mindfulness and concentration, and pronounce the fourth mantra: "Darling, I suffer so much. Please help me." This can be difficult, but you can do it. It just takes some training. When you suffer, you tend to want to be alone. Even if the other person tries to approach and to reconcile, you're reluctant to let go of your anger. This is very normal and human. But when we love each other, we *do* need each other, especially when we suffer. You believe that your suffering comes from him or her, but are you really so sure?

It's possible that you're wrong. Maybe he or she didn't intend to hurt you. Maybe you've misunderstood or have a wrong perception.

Don't rush into saying this mantra. When you're ready, go to the other person, breathe in and out deeply, and become yourself 100 percent. Then say the mantra with all your heart. You may not want to do it. You may want to say you don't need the other person. Your pride has been deeply hurt, after all. But don't let pride stand between you and the person you love. In true love there is no room for pride. If pride is still there, you know that you have to practice to transform your love into true love. Regularly practicing walking meditation, sitting meditation, and breathing in and out mindfully in order to restore yourself will also help train you so that you are prepared to use the fourth mantra the next time you suffer.

# five

# the power of stillness

I remember a time in Hue, Vietnam, in 1947, when I was living as a student at the Buddhist Institute of Bao Quoc Temple, not too far from my root temple (the temple where I had been ordained into monastic life and where I normally lived). At that time the French army occupied the whole region and had set up a military base in Hue. We often had gunfire around us between French and Vietnamese soldiers. People living high in the hills had set up small fortresses for protection. There were nights when the villagers shut themselves in their homes, bracing against the barrage. In the morning when they awoke, they sometimes found corpses from the battle of the previous night, with slogans written in whitewash mixed with blood on the road. Occasionally monks took the remote paths in this region, but hardly anyone else dared pass through the area—especially the city dwellers of Hue, who had only recently returned after having been evacuated. Even though Bao Quoc was situated near a train station, hardly anyone risked going there, which speaks for itself.

One morning I set out from Bao Quoc for my monthly visit back to my root temple. It was quite early; the dew was still on the tips of the grass. Inside a cloth bag I carried my ceremonial robe and a few sutras. In my hand, I carried the traditional Vietnamese cone-shaped hat. I felt light, and joyful at the thought of seeing my teacher, my monastic brothers, and the ancient, venerated temple.

I had just gone over a hill when I heard a voice call out. Up on the hill, above the road, I saw a French soldier waving. Thinking he was making fun of me because I was a monk, I turned away and continued walking down the road. But suddenly I had the feeling that this was no laughing matter. Behind me I heard the clomping of a soldier's boots running up behind me. Perhaps he wanted to search me; the cloth bag I was carrying could have looked suspicious to him. I stopped walking and waited. A young soldier with a thin, handsome face approached.

"Where are you going?" he asked in Vietnamese. From his pronunciation, I could tell that he was French and that his knowledge of Vietnamese was very limited.

I smiled and asked him in French, "If I were to reply in Vietnamese, would you understand?"

When he heard that I could speak French, his face lit up. He said he had no intention of searching me, and that he only wanted to ask me something. "I want to know which temple you're from," he said.

When I told him I was living at Bao Quoc Temple, he seemed interested.

"Bao Quoc Temple," he repeated. "Is that the big temple on the hill near the train station?"

When I nodded, he pointed up to a pump house on the side of the hill—his guard post, apparently—and said, "If you're not too busy, please come up there with me so we can talk for a little while." We sat down near the pump house and he told me about the visit he and five other soldiers had made ten days earlier to Bao Quoc Temple. They had gone to the temple at ten that night, in search of Vietnamese resistors, Vietminh, who were reportedly gathering there.

"We were determined to find them. We carried guns. The orders were to arrest and even kill if necessary. But when we entered the temple we were stunned."

"Because there were so many Vietminh?"

"No! No!" he exclaimed. "We wouldn't have been stunned if we had seen Vietminh. We would have attacked no matter how many there were."

I was confused. "What surprised you?"

"What happened was so unexpected. Whenever we did searches in the past, people would run away or be thrown into a state of panic."

"People have been terrorized so many times that they run away in fear," I explained.

"I myself don't make a habit of terrorizing or threatening people," he replied. "Perhaps it's because they have been harmed by those who came before us that they are so frightened.

"But when we entered the Bao Quoc Temple grounds, it was like entering a completely deserted place. The oil lamps were turned very low. We deliberately stomped our feet loudly on the gravel, and I had the feeling there were many people in the temple, but we couldn't hear anyone. It was incredibly quiet. The shouting of a comrade made me uneasy. No one replied. I turned on my flashlight and aimed it into the room we thought was empty—and I saw fifty or sixty monks sitting still and silent in meditation."

"That's because you came during our evening sitting period," I said, nodding my head.

"Yes. It was as if we'd run into a strange and invisible force," he said. "We were so taken aback that we turned and went back out to the courtyard. The monks just ignored us! They didn't raise a voice in reply, and they didn't show any sign of panic or fear."

"They weren't ignoring you; they were practicing concentrating on their breath—that was all."

"I felt drawn to their calmness," he admitted. "It really commanded my respect. We stood quietly in the courtyard at the foot of a large tree and waited for perhaps half an hour. Then a series of bells sounded, and the temple returned to normal activity. A monk lit a torch and came to invite us inside, but we simply told him why we were there and then took our leave. That day, I began to change my ideas about the Vietnamese people.

"There are many young men among us," he continued. "We are homesick; we miss our families and our country a lot. We have been sent here to kill the Vietminh, but we don't know if we will kill them or be killed by them and never return home to our families. Seeing the people here work so hard to rebuild their shattered lives reminds me of the shattered lives of my relatives in France. The peaceful and serene life of those monks makes me think about the lives of all human beings on this Earth. And I wonder why we've come to this place. What is this hatred between the Vietminh and us that we have traveled all the way over here to fight them?"

Deeply moved, I took his hand. I told him the story of an old friend of mine who had enlisted to fight the French, and who had been successful in winning many battles. One day my friend came to the temple where I was, and burst into tears as he embraced me. He told me that during an attack on a fortress, while he was concealed behind some rocks, he saw two young French soldiers sitting and talking. "When I saw the bright, handsome, innocent faces of those boys," he said, "I couldn't bear to open fire, dear Brother. People can label me weak and soft; they can say that if all the Vietnamese fighters were like me, it wouldn't be long before our whole country was overtaken. But for a moment I loved the enemy like my own mother loves me! I knew that the death of these two youngsters would make their mothers in France suffer, just as my mother had grieved for the death of my younger brother."

"So you see," I said to this Frenchman, "that young Vietnamese soldier's heart was filled with the love of humanity."

The young French soldier sat quietly, lost in thought. Perhaps, like me, he was becoming more aware of the absurdity of the killing, the calamity of war, and the suffering of so many young people dying in an unjust and heartbreaking way.

The sun had already risen high in the sky and it was time for me to go. The soldier told me that his name was Daniel Marty and he was twenty-one years old. He had just finished high school before he came to Vietnam. He showed me photographs of his mother, and a younger brother and sister. We parted with a feeling of understanding between us, and he promised to visit me at the temple on Sundays.

In the months that followed, he did visit me when he could, and I took him to our meditation hall to practice with me. I gave him the spiritual name Thanh Luong, meaning "pure and refreshing peaceful life." I taught him Vietnamese—he knew only the few phrases that he'd been taught by the military—and after a few months we were able to converse a little in my native tongue. He told me that he no longer had to go on raids as he had previously done, and I shared his relief. If there were letters from home, he showed them to me. Whenever he saw me, he joined his palms in greeting.

One day, we invited Thanh Luong to a vegetarian meal at the temple. He accepted the invitation happily, and highly praised the delicious black olives and the flavorful dishes we served him. He found the fragrant mushroom rice soup my brother had prepared so delicious, he couldn't believe it was vegetarian. I had to explain to him in detail how it was made before he would believe it.

There were days when, sitting beside the temple tower, we would delve into conversations on spirituality and literature. When I praised French literature, Thanh Luong's eyes lit up with pride in his nation's culture. Our friendship became very deep.

Then one day, when he came to visit, Thanh Luong announced that his unit would be moving to another area and it was likely that he would soon be able to return to France.

I walked him to the gate under the arch of the three

portals of the temple and we hugged good-bye. "I will write you, Brother," he said.

"I will be very happy to receive your letter, and to reply."

A month later, I received a letter from him with the news that he would indeed return to France, but then go on to Algeria. He promised to write to me from there. I have not heard from him since. Who knows where Thanh Luong is now. Is he safe? But I know that when I last saw him, he was at peace. That moment of profound silence in the temple had changed him. He allowed the lives of all living beings to fill his heart, and he saw the meaninglessness and destructiveness of war. What made it all possible was that moment of complete and total *stopping* and opening to the powerful, healing, miraculous ocean called silence.

To manifest our true nature, we need to bring a stop to the constant internal conversation that takes up all the space in us. We can start by turning off Radio NST for little moments each day, in order to give that mental space over to joy instead.

## a  m i n d f u l  b r e a t h

As we've already seen, the easiest way to free ourselves from the endless wheel of nonstop thinking is by learning the practice of mindful breathing. We breathe all the time, but we rarely pay attention to our breathing. We rarely *enjoy* our breathing.

A mindful breath is the treat you get to enjoy when you're giving all your attention to your in-breath and out-breath for the full length of that inhalation and exhalation. If you pay attention as you breathe, it's as though all the cells in your brain and in the rest of your body are singing the same song.

*With the act of breathing in mindfully,*

*you go inside. Your body is breathing;*

*and your body is your home.*

*In each breath, you can come*

*home to yourself.*

—

You may have a lot of sadness, anger, or loneliness in you. When you connect with your in-breath and out-breath, you can get in touch with those feelings without fear of becoming their prisoner. Your mindful breathing is a way of saying, "Don't worry, I am right here at home; I will take care of this feeling."

Your mindful breath is your home base. If you want to realize your aspirations; if you want to build connection with your family and friends; if you want to help your community—you need to begin with your breath. Every breath, every step, every action done in mindfulness will give you sustenance.

## making space for mindfulness is easier than you think

Many of us think there's no room in our life for cultivating mindfulness. But the truth is that mindful living is more a matter of reorienting yourself, of remembering your true intention, than of squeezing an additional event called "Meditation" into your daily agenda. You don't have to be in your meditation room or wait until you have an unscheduled hour to practice mindfulness, although these are certainly wonderful things to enjoy whenever you're able. Quiet, mindful breathing is something you can do at any time. Wherever you are can be a sacred space, if you are there in a relaxed and serene way, following your breathing and keeping your concentration on whatever you're doing.

When you wake up in the morning, while you're still in bed, you can start the day with a mindful breath. Take that moment, first thing, to follow your breathing in and out and be aware that you have twenty-four brand-new hours to live. This is a gift of life!

After I was ordained as a novice monk, I had to memorize many short verses to help me practice mindfulness. The first verse I learned goes like this:

> *Waking up this morning I smile.*
> *Twenty-four brand-new hours are before me.*
> *I vow to live them deeply*
> *and learn to look at everything around me with the*
> *eyes of compassion.*

As you can see, there are four lines. The first line is for your in-breath. The second line is for your out-breath. The third line is for your next in-breath. And the fourth line is for your out-breath. As you breathe, you use the verse to focus your attention on the sacred dimension of what you're doing. You want to live the twenty-four hours that are given you in such a way that peace and happiness are possible. You are determined not to waste your twenty-four hours, because you know that those twenty-four hours are a gift of life, and you receive that gift anew every morning.

If you can sit comfortably, sitting meditation is a wonderful way to practice mindful breathing. Many people cannot allow themselves the time to sit and do nothing but breathe. They consider it to be uneconomical or a luxury. People say "time is money." But time is much more than money. Time is *life*. The simple practice of sitting quietly on a regular basis can be profoundly healing. Stopping and sitting is a good way to focus on mindful breathing and nothing else.

Just as you can choose to turn off the television when you eat, you can turn off Radio Non-Stop Thinking at mealtimes by paying attention to your breath, your food, and the people you're eating with. When you're cleaning the kitchen or washing dishes, you can do those tasks in an awakened way, in a spirit of love, joy, and gratitude. When you brush your teeth, you can choose to do it in mindfulness. Don't think of other things; just focus your attention on brushing your teeth.

You spend maybe two or three minutes brushing your teeth. During that time, you can be mindful of your teeth and of your brushing. Brushing your teeth like that can bring happiness. When you go to the toilet, it's also possible to enjoy that time. Mindfulness can change your relationship to everything. It can help you be truly present and really enjoy whatever you are doing.

Practicing mindful walking is another opportunity to create moments of happiness and to heal, as we saw earlier. Every time you take a step, as you breathe in and out, you can relish the sensation of your feet making contact with the earth. When you take a step in mindfulness, you come back to yourself. Each step helps you connect with your body. It brings you home to the here and now. So when you walk from the parking lot or the bus stop to your workplace, when you walk to the post office or grocery store, why not go *home* with every step?

In any activity, every time you're quiet and aware, you have the chance to connect with yourself. Most of the time, we walk and we don't know that we're walking. We're standing there, but we don't know that we're there; our mind is miles away. We're alive, but we don't know that we're *alive*. We're continually losing ourselves. So quieting your body and mind and sitting just to be with yourself is an act of revolution. You sit down and you stop that state of vacancy—of losing yourself, of not being yourself. When you sit down, you can come back and connect with yourself. You don't need an iPhone or a computer to do that. You just need to sit down mindfully and breathe in and out mindfully, and in a few seconds you're back in touch with yourself. You know what's going on—what's going on in your body, in your feelings, in your emotions, and in your perceptions. You are already home, and you can take good care of home.

Perhaps you have been away from home for a long time, and home has become a mess. How many mistakes have you made as a result of ignoring how your body was feeling, what emotions were coming up inside, what erroneous perceptions were driving your thinking and your speech?

Truly going home means sitting down and being with yourself, reconnecting with yourself, and accepting the situation as it is. Even if it is a mess, you can accept it—and that is the starting point for reorienting yourself so you can move forward in a more positive direction. I think often of Thanh Luong, who was able to have that moment of deep silence in the temple and then bring it back with him into the chaos of war.

Even if we are deep in our own particular kind of chaos, we can always find space for some silence each day that helps us find peace in the situation as it is—and may even show us a new path out of the mess.

Once I held a retreat at a monastery in the mountains of Northern California. At the beginning of the retreat, there was a large wildfire nearby. While we were practicing sitting and walking meditation, we could hear the sound of many helicopters. It wasn't exactly a pleasant sound. Many of the practitioners, including myself, were either Vietnamese or Vietnamese-American, and for us the sound of helicopters meant guns, death, bombs, and more death. We had lived through a brutal war and it was disturbing to hear the helicopters all the time and be reminded of that violence. Even for those people at the retreat who hadn't experienced war, the sound was still loud and intrusive.

But the helicopters were not leaving, and neither were we. So we chose to practice listening to the sound of the helicopters with mindfulness. Hearing a pleasant sound, like that of a bell, people *want* to focus their attention on it. Giving our attention to a pleasant sound, it's easy to feel more present and happy. Now we had to learn how to focus positively with the sound of helicopters. With mindfulness, we were able to remind our reactive selves that this was not a helicopter operating in a situation of war. This helicopter was helping to extinguish destructive flames. With that awareness, we could transform an unpleasant feeling into a feeling of gratitude and appreciation. Because the sound of those helicopters came along as often as every couple of minutes, if we didn't practice mindfulness in that way, it could be quite tedious.

So everyone—there were close to six hundred people at the retreat—practiced breathing in and out with the sound of the helicopters. We said to ourselves the verse for listening to the bell, which we modified to fit the situation:

*I listen.*
*I listen.*
*This helicopter sound*
*brings me back to the present moment.*

And we survived very well. We made the helicopter sound into something helpful.

## five minutes for life

If you're just starting out, try dedicating five minutes every day to walking quietly and mindfully. When you are alone, you can do it as slowly as you like. You may find it helpful to begin by walking very slowly, taking one step with each in-breath, one step with each out-breath. As you breathe in, you make one step; and you walk in such a way that with that one step, that one in-breath, your thinking mind can come totally to a stop. If it hasn't fully stopped, then just pause, and stay there mindfully breathing in and out until you have completely stopped your thinking. You will feel it. In a state of mindful being, something really does change physically and mentally.

If you succeed in making one step like that, then you know that you can make two steps like that. You begin with just five minutes, but you may find yourself enjoying it so much that you like doing it several times a day.

People are so busy. We are always pulled away from the present moment. We have no chance to live our life truly. Mindfulness can recognize that. That is enlightenment already. So we start from that enlightenment, that awakening: we really want to live our own life, we really want to stop—not to be carried away from life. And with the practice of mindful sitting and breathing, walking, or indeed even brushing our teeth, we *can* stop. The practice of stopping can be realized at any time of the day—including when we're driving a car.

*You are released; you gain freedom.*

*And with that kind of freedom,*

*with that kind of release, healing*

*becomes possible. Life becomes*

*possible. Joy becomes possible.*

———————

People talk nowadays about work-life balance. We tend to think of work as one thing and life as another, separate thing; but it doesn't have to be that way. After you drive to work and park your car in the parking lot, you can choose between walking mind-

fully and happily to your office, or walking distract-
edly and in a hurry. You have to walk that distance
anyway. If you know *how* to walk, how to be there
for yourself as you walk, then from the parking lot
to your office every step can bring you joy and happiness. You can release the tension in your body with
every step. You can touch the wonders of life with
every step.

When you walk mindfully, you invest 100 percent of yourself in the walking. You become aware
of every step: it's *you* who are consciously walking;
it's not the habit energy pulling you. You retain your
sovereignty. You are the king or queen who decides.
You walk because it is your intention to walk, and in
every step you have freedom. You take each step pur-
posefully, and each mindful step brings you in touch
with the wonders of life that are available in the here
and now. Walking like that, you invest the entirety of
your body and your mind in every step. That is why,
when walking, you do not think. If you think, the
thinking will steal your walking from you. You do
not talk, because talking will take the walking away
from you.

Walking like that is a pleasure. When mindfulness
and concentration are alive in you, you are fully your-

self; you don't lose yourself. You walk like a buddha.
Without mindfulness, you may think of walking as an
imposition, a chore. With mindfulness, you see walking as life.

Similarly, when you wash dishes after dinner, it is
*how* you wash the dishes that determines whether it is
drudgery or whether it is a moment of real life. There
is a way to wash dishes that helps you enjoy every
minute. When you mop the floor, when you cook your
breakfast—if you know how to do it in mindfulness,
then it's *life*, not *work*.

People who are fixated on separating life from
work spend the majority of their lives not living. We
need to find ways to bring mindfulness, space, and
joy into *all* our activities, not just when we're doing
something that seems like play or like meditating. If
we bring mindfulness into each part of our day, five
minutes at a time, our imagined divide between life
and work disappears, and every part of our day is
time for ourselves.

## practice:
## walking meditation

People say it is a miracle to walk on air, on water, or on fire. But for me, walking peacefully on Earth is the real miracle. Mother Earth herself is a miracle. Each step is a miracle. Taking conscious steps on our beautiful planet can bring healing and happiness. Walking meditation is a wonderful way to come back to the present moment and come back to life.

When you practice walking meditation, be fully aware of your foot, the ground, and the connection between them. Let your breathing be natural; and match your steps to your breath, not the other way around. Take a few steps for each in-breath and a few steps for each out-breath. The out-breath tends to be longer, so you may need more steps for it. At certain times and in appropriate places, perhaps where there aren't too many people, it can be especially healing to walk slowly, taking one step for each in-breath and one step for each out-breath. With each in- and out-breath, say, "In" then "Out," or "Arrived" then "Home." With every step you will arrive in your true home, the present moment.

If you feel lost, if you're in the midst of a chaotic situation, or even if you're just feeling a little bit lazy, don't worry: you don't need to make any effort to practice mindful breathing, sitting, or walking. The breathing itself is enough; the sitting is enough; the walking is enough. Let yourself become one with the action. Just be the walking.

One day in 2003 I was in Korea, about to lead a walking meditation through the streets of Seoul. Many people had come to join the walk. But because there were so many photographers and reporters jammed together shoulder to shoulder directly in front of us, I found it impossible to begin. I said, "Dear Buddha, I give up. Please, *you* walk for me." I took one step. Right away a path opened up and I was able to continue. After this experience, I wrote the following verses. I still use them in my practice of walking meditation. Perhaps they will help you too.

*Let the Buddha breathe.*
*Let the Buddha walk.*

*I don't have to breathe.*
*I don't have to walk.*

*The Buddha is breathing.*
*The Buddha is walking.*

*I enjoy the breathing.*
*I enjoy the walking.*

*There is only the breathing.*
*There is only the walking.*

*There is no breather.*
*There is no walker.*

# six

paying attention

The more often we're able to practice coming home to ourselves, and the more time we spend in mindfulness, the more we are going to become aware of our own suffering. Even though mindful breathing and quiet do put us in touch with joy, they are also likely to bring us in contact with pain (especially at first) as we become more conscious of the suffering we have been hiding from.

We have a natural tendency to want to run away from suffering. But without any suffering, we can't fully develop as human beings.

When we approach suffering in that way, we actually end up suffering much less, and the suffering can transform itself more easily.

If instead we continue to try to run away from suffering, to push it into the furthermost corners of our mind, we only perpetuate it.

*If we never suffer, there is no basis or*

*impetus for developing understanding*

*and compassion. Suffering is very*

*important. We have to learn to*

*recognize and even embrace suffering,*

*as our awareness of it helps us grow.*

Quite often we avoid silence, thinking that we will thereby avoid suffering; but in truth, taking quiet time to come home to ourselves with awareness is the only thing that will help heal our suffering.

## recognizing suffering

Much of my teaching is aimed at helping people learn how to recognize suffering, embrace it, and transform it. That is an art. We have to be able to smile to our suffering with peace, just as we smile to the mud because we know that it's only when we have mud (and know how to make good use of the mud) that we can grow lotus flowers.

There can be big sources of suffering, major emotional hurts that stay with us long past the original wound. But there are also what in French we call *les petites misères,* the little sufferings that can wear us down day after day. If we know how to handle these little miseries, we don't have to become a victim of the so-called daily grind. When suffering has become a block— whether from major hurts or *les petites misères*—we should know how to recognize it and embrace it.

The suffering we feel may have been transmitted to us by our father, our mother, our ancestors. When we are able to recognize, embrace, and transform it, we do that not only for ourselves, but also for our father, our mother, and our ancestors.

Pain is inescapable. It is everywhere. Besides our

individual and collective suffering as human beings, there is suffering in nature as well. Natural and unnatural disasters happen daily around the globe—tsunamis, wildfires, famines, wars. Innocent children die every day due to the lack of clean water, or food, or medicine. We are connected to these sufferings, even if we don't experience them directly. That little baby, that old woman, that young man or young woman—when they die, in some way it's also we who are dying. And yet at the same time we are of course still living, so that means that they are somehow still living as well. This is a meditation. Understanding this deep truth can help us develop our volition, our desire to live in a way that can help others stay alive as well.

## island of self

When we walk into our own home, we can relax, let our hair down, and just be ourselves. We feel warm, comfortable, safe, and content. Home is a place where loneliness can disappear.

But where is home, really?

*Our true home is what the Buddha*

*called the island of self, the peaceful*

*place inside of us. Oftentimes we*

*don't notice it's there; we don't even*

*really know where we are, because*

*our outer or inner environment*

*is filled with noise. We need some*

*quietness to find that island of self.*

———————

Every time you feel unwell, agitated, sad, afraid, or worried—these are times to use mindful breathing to go back home to your island of mindfulness. If you regularly practice mindfulness, going back to your island at the times when you *aren't* experiencing difficulty, then when you do have a problem it will be much easier and more enjoyable to find that safe place and go home again. You are fortunate enough to know the practice of mindfulness; please make good use of the practice to strengthen the connection to your true home. Do not wait until you are hit by a giant wave to try to go back to your island. Practice going back as often as you can by living the ordinary moments of your life mindfully. Then when, inevitably, difficult moments in life do arrive, going home will be natural and easy to do.

Walking, breathing, sitting, eating, and drinking tea in mindfulness—all these are concrete practices of taking refuge that you can enjoy many times every day. You have the seed of mindfulness in you; that seed is always there. Your in-breath and out-breath are always available. You have the island within yourself. Taking refuge on that island through mindfulness is a matter of daily practice.

## the coconut monk

There was a monk in Vietnam who was called the Coconut Monk because he liked to climb up a coconut tree onto a platform, where he would practice sitting meditation. It was cooler up there. As a young man, he had studied in France and had become an engineer. But when he returned to Vietnam, where war was raging everywhere, he no longer wanted to be an engineer; he wanted to be a monk, and he practiced as a monk. He wrote a letter in honor of Nhat Chi Mai, a lay student of mine who had immolated herself to call for an end to the war. He said, "I am burning myself like you. The only difference is that I am burning myself more slowly." He was saying that his life was also given over entirely to calling for peace.

The Coconut Monk did many things to teach peace. One time he organized a practice center in the Mekong Delta and asked many people to come and practice sitting meditation with him. He collected bullets and bomb fragments from the area and forged them into a big bell, a bell of mindfulness. He hung it in his practice center and invited the bell to sound day and night. He wrote a poem in which he said: "Dear bullets, dear bombs, I have helped you come together in order to practice. In your former life you have killed and destroyed. But in this life you are calling out to people to wake up, to wake up to humanity, to love, to understanding." He invited that bell every night and every morning. The bell's very existence was a symbol of how transformation was possible.

One day he went to the presidential palace, wanting to deliver a message of peace. The guards wouldn't allow him to enter. When talking with them didn't work, the monk became silent. He settled in and slept just outside the palace gate. He had brought a cage with him, and in that cage were a mouse and a cat who had learned to be friends. The cat did not eat the mouse. One guard asked him, "What is your purpose in being here?" The Coconut Monk said, "I want to show the president that even a cat and a mouse can live peacefully together." He wanted everyone to ask themselves: If even cat and mouse can live in peace, why not we humans?

The Coconut Monk spent a lot of time alone and in silence. His volition, his desire, was to be part of creating a more peaceful environment for the country; and to do that he needed to be very clear and not distracted. Some people might say he was crazy. But I don't think he was. I think he was an activist for peace who was very solidly at home in the island of himself.

## solitude

When people hear the phrase "the island of self," they often think it means they have to live alone and have to shut people and everything else out of their life. But this practice, this kind of "living alone," doesn't mean there's no one around you. It only means that you are established firmly in the here and now; you are aware of everything that is happening in the present moment.

You use your mindfulness to become aware of everything, of every feeling, every perception in yourself, as well as what's happening around you in your community. You are always with yourself; you don't lose yourself. That is the deeper way of living a life of solitude.

To practice solitude is to practice being in this singular moment, not caught in the past, not carried away by the future, and most of all, not carried away by the crowd. You don't have to go to the forest. You can live with people, you can go to the grocery store, you can walk with others—and you can still enjoy silence and solitude. In today's society, with so many things around you clamoring for your attention and your reaction, that inner solitude is something you have to learn.

It is good to spend some time physically alone each day as well. You might think that you can be joyful only when you are with other people, talking and laughing and playing around. But joy and happiness can be very great in solitude as well—so deep that you are more able to share. If you have deep joy and happiness, developed in solitude, then you have a lot to give. Without the capacity for being alone, you become more and more depleted. And when you don't have enough nourishment for yourself, you don't have much to offer others. That's why learning to live in solitude is important.

Each day, devote some time to being physically alone, because that makes it easier to practice nourishing yourself and looking deeply. That doesn't mean it's impossible to practice being alone and looking deeply when you're with a crowd of people. It *is* possible. Even if you're sitting in the marketplace, you can be alone and not be carried away by the crowd. You are still yourself, still the master of yourself. Likewise, you can still be yourself even if you are in a lively group discussion and even if there is a strong collective emotion.

generations of ancestors, and we continue to reinforce it. It is very powerful. We are intelligent enough to know that if we do this particular thing, if we make that accusatory remark, we will cause damage in our relationship. We don't want to make that remark or do that thing, yet when we find ourselves in a tense situation, we say or do the very thing we know will be destructive. Why? Because it's stronger than we are. Habit energy pushes us all the time. That is why mindfulness practice aims at liberating ourselves from habit energy.

I remember sitting on the bus one day in India with a friend; we were visiting Dalit communities. Together, we traveled to many Indian states to offer days of mindfulness practice and public lectures and retreats. The landscape outside the window of the bus was beautiful, with palm trees, temples, buffalo, and rice fields. I was enjoying looking at everything, but my friend seemed very tense; clearly he was not enjoying it as I was. He was struggling. I said, "My dear friend, there is nothing for you to worry about now. I know that your concern is to make my trip pleasant, and to make me happy; but I *am* happy right now, so enjoy yourself. Sit back; smile. The landscape is very beautiful."

He said, "Okay," and he sat more comfortably in his seat. But when I looked over at him again just a few minutes later, he was as tense as before. He was still worrying, fretting, and fidgeting. He couldn't let go of the struggle, that struggle that had been going on for many thousands of years. He was not capable of dwelling in the present moment and touching life deeply in that moment, which was my practice, and still is my practice. You see, he had been an untouchable himself. Now he had a family, a beautiful apartment to live in, and a good job, but he still carried all the habit energy, the suffering of all his ancestors in the past many thousands of years. He struggled during the day and he struggled during the night, even in his dreams. He was not capable of letting go and relaxing.

Our ancestors may have been luckier than his were, but many of us are haunted and restless just the same. We do not allow ourselves to relax, to be in the here and now. Why must we run and run, even when we're preparing our breakfast, even while eating our lunch, while walking, while sitting? There is something pushing us, pulling us, all the time. What are we running toward?

The Buddha addressed this issue very clearly. He said, "Don't agonize over the past, because the past is gone. Don't worry about the future, because the future is not yet here. There is only one moment for you to be alive, and that is the present moment. Come back to the present moment and live this moment deeply, and you'll be free."

## untying the two knots

There are two kinds of knots. The first consists of our notions and ideas, our concepts and knowledge. Everyone has notions and ideas; but when we get stuck in them, we're not free, and we have no chance to touch the truth in life. The second kind of knot is our afflictions and habits of suffering, such as fear, anger, discrimination, despair, arrogance. They must be removed in order for us to be free.

These two knots, which are etched deeply into our brain and consciousness, bind us and push us to do things we don't want to do; they make us say things we don't want to say. So we're not free. Any time we do things not from our true desire but out of habitual fear or ingrained notions and ideas, we're not free.

When you read this book, when you meditate, it's

not for the purpose of getting notions and ideas. In fact, it is for releasing notions and ideas. Don't just replace your old notions and ideas with a newer set. Stop chasing one notion of happiness after another, exchanging one idea for another.

We all have patterns of behavior, habit energies that can run very deep. Every day we allow these unseen energies to govern our lives. We act, and react, under the influence of these tendencies in us. But our minds are naturally flexible. As neuroscientists say, our brains have plasticity. We can transform them.

*Being able to stop and be aware of the present moment is part of the definition of happiness. It is not possible to be happy in the future. This is not a matter of belief; this is a matter of experience.*

When we stop the body, the mental chatter seems louder. When we stop the mental chatter, the constant cognitive agitation, we can experience a spaciousness that allows us a chance to live our life in a radically new and satisfying way.

We can't be happy without space for silence. I know this from direct observation and experience; I don't need a neuroscientist's machine to tell me. When I see someone walking by, I can generally tell whether this person is happy or not happy, peaceful or not peaceful, loving or not loving. Without silence, we aren't living in the present moment, and this moment is our very best chance to find happiness.

## angulimala

In the time of the Buddha there lived a man called Angulimala. He was a notorious serial killer. He suffered a great deal and he was full of hate.

One day he entered a town, and all the people panicked. As it happened, the Buddha and his community were staying nearby, and the Buddha came into that same town on his morning alms-round. One of the townspeople implored him, "Dear teacher, it's so dangerous to walk out there on the road! Come into our house. Let me offer you something to eat. Angulimala is in town."

The Buddha said, "That's all right. My practice is to walk outside and to visit not just one house but many houses. I am here not only to find my daily meal but also to get in touch with people, to give them an opportunity to practice giving as they feel moved to, and to offer them teachings." So the Buddha did not accede to his follower's anxious plea. He had enough peace, spiritual strength, and courage to continue his practice. It also happened to be the case that before becoming a monk, he had been an excellent practitioner of martial arts.

The Buddha held his bowl with peace and concentration, and he walked mindfully, enjoying every step. Then after his alms-round was completed, as he was walking through the forest, he heard the sound of someone running up from behind him. He realized that it was Angulimala. This was the first time that Angulimala had seen a person without fear. Anybody else approached by Angulimala tried to run away as fast as they could, except those most unfortunate ones who were literally paralyzed by fear.

But with the Buddha the situation was very different. He simply kept on walking, unperturbed. Angulimala was enraged to see someone so completely unfazed by him. The Buddha was mindful; he was aware of the situation. But his pulse was stable, and there was no adrenaline pumping through his system. He was not frantically weighing whether to fight or to flee. He was composed. He had a good practice!

When Angulimala had nearly caught up, he called out, "Monk, monk! Stop!" But the Buddha continued to walk calmly, serenely, nobly. He was the embodiment of peace, of nonfear. Angulimala came up alongside the Buddha and said, "Monk, why don't you stop? I told you to stop!"

Still walking, the Buddha said, "Angulimala, I have stopped for a long time already. It is you who have not stopped."

Angulimala was stunned. "What do you mean? You are still walking, and you say that you have stopped?"

Then the Buddha told Angulimala what it means to really stop. The Buddha said, "Angulimala, it's not good to go on as you are doing. You know that you are causing a lot of suffering to yourself as well as to many other people. You have to learn how to love."

"Love? You're talking to me about love? Human beings are very cruel. I hate them all. I want to kill them all. Love does not exist."

The Buddha said gently, "Angulimala, I know that you have suffered a great deal, and your anger, your hate is very big. But if you look around, you can see kind, loving people. Have you met any of the monks and nuns in my community? Have you met any of my lay students? They are very compassionate, very peaceful; no one can deny it. You should not blind yourself to the truth that there is love, that there are people who are capable of love. Angulimala, stop."

Angulimala replied, "It's too late; it's much too late now for me to stop. Even if I tried, people would not allow me to. They would slay me in an instant. I can't ever stop if I want to survive."

The Buddha said, "Dear friend, it's never too late. Stop now. I'll help you as a friend. And our sangha will protect you." Upon hearing that, Angulimala cast off his sword, knelt down, and asked to be accepted into the sangha, the community of the Buddha. He became the most diligent practitioner in the community. He transformed totally and became an utterly gentle person, the embodiment of nonviolence.

If Angulimala could stop, then all of us can do it. None of us is more busy, more anxious, more crazed than this murderer was. We can't find the peace of silence without stopping. Running faster and faster, pushing ourselves harder, will never bring it within our reach. We won't find it anywhere but *here*. The moment we're able to really stop, both the movement and the internal noise, we begin to find a healing silence. Silence is not a deprivation, an empty void. The more space we make for stillness and silence, the more we have to give both to ourselves and to others.

# practice:
# the island of self

When the Buddha was stricken with his last illness, he knew that many of his disciples would feel lost when he died. So he taught them to not rely on anything outside themselves, but to take refuge in the island of self. When you practice conscious breathing and produce mindfulness in yourself, you go back and discover the teacher within, pointing you toward the island of self.

Your island contains birds, trees, and streams, just like the mainland. There's ultimately no real dividing line between inside and outside. If you're not *there*, if you're not truly yourself on your island, there can be no real contact with the world outside. Getting in touch deeply with the inside, you get in touch with the outside also, and vice versa. Genuine connection is possible only when you have enough mindfulness and concentration. So going back to your island means first of all generating mindfulness and concentration.

In Plum Village, we have a song called "The Island of Self." You might like to use it as a guided meditation as you sit or walk in mindfulness.

*Breathing in,*
*I go back*
*to the island*
*within myself.*

*There are beautiful trees*
*within the island.*
*There are clear streams*
*of water; there are birds,*
*sunshine, and fresh air.*

*Breathing out,*
*I feel safe.*
*I enjoy going back*
*to my island.*

seven

cultivating connection

Never in the history of humankind have we had so many means of communication—cell phones, texting, e-mail, online social media—but we are more distant from each other than ever. There is remarkably little true communication between family members, between members of a society, between nations.

As a civilization we surely have not cultivated the arts of listening and speaking to a satisfactory degree. We don't know how to really listen to each other. Most of us have precious little ability to express ourselves or listen to others with openness and sincerity. When we can't communicate, energy gets blocked inside and it makes us sick; and as our sickness increases, we suffer, and our suffering spills over onto other people.

If we want to be more connected to others, we don't need to text them more; we need to listen to them more. Deep listening leads to understanding. Understanding leads to greater connection. The way to listen more deeply is not simply to try harder. Rather, it is to take time in practice that starts with silence—that is, with quieting our internal Radio Non-Stop Thinking.

## staying connected through mindfulness

We all crave connection, and many of us try to find it through our phones or e-mail. We feel a neurochemical sweetness when someone sends us a text or an e-mail, and we feel anxious when we're not with our phones or near them.

I don't have a telephone, but I don't feel disconnected from my friends and students. I think about them frequently. I write them letters on real paper with a real pen. It takes a while—sometimes a few days or a week—for me to write a one-page letter to a friend. But during that time, I have a lot of time to think about that friend! I have friends who come visit too. We don't talk as often as if they were calling me on the phone, but when we are together we really value that shared time. I watch them and listen to them carefully; their words are precious because I will not hear them again for a while.

Have you ever been with the kind of good friend with whom you don't even need to speak? To me that is the deepest kind of friendship: a spiritual friendship. It is something very rare. A good spiritual friend is in a certain sense your teacher. A real teacher is someone who has freedom and no fear of silence. That person need not be *called* a teacher, and he or she may be younger than you. If in your life you have even one good spiritual friend, you are very fortunate. It's said that to meet a good spiritual friend is something as rare as the opening of the udumbara flower, an event that happens only every three thousand years. (The udumbara flower's botanical name is *Ficus glomerata;* the plant belongs to the fig family.)

When we meet a good spiritual friend, we have to know how to benefit from that friend. That person has awakened understanding, happiness, and freedom; and we can take refuge in him or her while we water our own seeds of awakened understanding and freedom. We will find in the end that we don't need emotional or material comforts much. We don't need our spiritual friend to compliment us or to phone us every day. We don't need store-bought presents or any special treatment from that friend.

We have to use our time well. If we waste our time with trivial expectations, we won't be able to profit from the true gifts of spiritual friends. We can gain valuable wisdom by observing how they behave in different circumstances. We can experience for ourselves the awakened understanding that they enjoy. We don't have to sit next to them all day long, or press them to acknowledge us and give us attention. We can simply savor their presence without needing them to do or give us anything.

A good spiritual friend could be anyone; it might not be the person you'd expect. But when you find a friend like this, it's a great happiness.

# nurturing a loving silence

If you live with someone, you may know the kind of comfortable silence that comes from being used to one another. But if you don't take care, this comfort can cause you to take the other person for granted. Antoine de Saint-Exupéry, the author of *The Little Prince,* wrote, "Love does not consist in gazing at each other but in looking outward in the same direction." I don't think sitting in a room together staring at the TV is what he had in mind!

Maybe the reason we're both staring at the TV is because looking at each other doesn't bring as much happiness as it once did. When we first met, we thought our beloved was delightful. He or she was the angel of our life, and we said, "I can't live without you." Hearing each other's voices was like hearing sweet birdsong; seeing each other was like the sun coming out. Now, looking at each other and hearing each other no longer brings us joy. Maybe we've had too many arguments and not known how to reconcile and find our happiness again. If we keep watching the TV instead of finding a way to reconnect, things will only get worse with each passing year.

One time a woman came to interview the sisters of New Hamlet in Plum Village for the French edition of *Elle* magazine. One day, as the journalist was talking with them, I came by to visit, so she took that opportunity to interview me. She wanted me to talk about meditation and mindfulness. But I felt inspired to offer a different sort of practical exercise. This is what I proposed to the readers of *Elle* as a practice:

This evening after your meal, when your husband turns on the television, practice breathing in deeply, calming your body and your mind, and then say to him with a smile, "Darling, would you mind turning off the TV? I have something I'd like to talk with you about." With loving speech, you address him like that. He may be a little annoyed. He's waiting for you to start a quarrel or something like that.

After he turns off the TV, you continue smiling and say, "Darling, why aren't we happy as a couple? It seems like we have everything. We both have good salaries, we have a beautiful house and enough money in the bank. So why aren't we happy? Can we take a few minutes to reflect on that? We started out very well; there

was happiness. Can we talk together to find out
the reason our happiness is gone, and can we
find a way to make things better?"

That's meditation. That's real meditation. Normally
we just blame the other person, but in any relationship *both* people are co-responsible for the course it
takes. Neither partner knows how to nourish love and
happiness. Most of us don't know how to handle suffering, or help another person handle suffering. So, I
told those *Elle* readers, for the sharing to be useful and
good, you have to be prepared to say something like, "I
have made mistakes. I have thought, spoken, and acted
in ways that have harmed our happiness and damaged
our connection."

When we find ourselves struggling in a relationship,
we need to come back to ourselves and take a close
look. If we can recognize where our way of thinking,
speaking, and acting has been detrimental to the relationship, we can tell the other person we're sorry. With
sincerity and mindfulness, we can express our desire to
begin anew.

The practice I described to the journalist can be
done in every home. It starts with our turning off the
television and sharing. Using normal language, we

look deeply together into our situation. You might like to initiate such a conversation yourself.

When a couple is suffering and they're looking in the same direction, it shouldn't be the direction of the television. True lovers should look in the direction of peace. We all need to practice nourishing our love and helping each other handle the suffering that is there in ourselves, in our partner and friends, and in the world. People are suffering all around us, and we have to offer our support. This is possible to do. And whenever we help people suffer less, our happiness grows.

In Plum Village retreats, there are always couples in attendance who are at the point of breaking up. Signing up for the retreat is their last resort. And every time after a retreat of five, six, or seven days, there are always partners who are able to reconcile. That nourishes everyone's happiness.

You and your partner are lovers; you can dream, think, and act in ways that help others suffer much less. Once you know how to nourish happiness and handle suffering in yourself and in your partner, the two of you can go on to help others. That is looking in the same direction. That consolidates and increases your happiness.

## the music of silence

In music there are moments of "rest," of no sound. If those spaces weren't there, it would be a mess. Music without moments of silence would be chaotic and oppressive. When we can sit quietly with a friend without saying anything, it's as precious and important as the resting notes we need in music. Silence shared among friends can be even better than talking.

Trinh Cong Son was a beloved singer-songwriter born in 1939. He has been called "the Bob Dylan of Vietnam." It's said that when he died in 2001, hundreds of thousands of people gathered for a spontaneous funeral concert. That would make it the highest-attendance event in Vietnamese history after the funeral procession of Ho Chi Minh.

Trinh Cong Son was fatigued by noisiness, even when it was shouts of praise and applause. He cherished the silent moments. He wrote: "There are some friends whose presence is like the resting notes in music. It gives a sense of ease, freedom, bliss. You don't have to make meaningless small talk. You feel totally yourself and comfortable." Trinh Cong Son relished those times when he could just sit with a friend without having to do or even say anything and just be nourished by friendship. All of us need friendships like that.

In Plum Village we love to do sitting meditation, especially as a community, as a spiritual family. During sitting meditation we don't talk, yet many of us feel that sitting with three or four people or more is more joyful than doing sitting meditation alone. Sitting in stillness together like that, everyone is nourished by each other's presence.

The classic "Lute Song" of ancient traditional Vietnamese music tells the story of a woman who is playing the lute and then, at a certain moment, stops. The song says: "*Thu thoi vo thanh thang huu thanh.*" *Thu thoi* means "right now." *Vo thanh* means "absence of sound." *Thang* means "to triumph over," and *huu thanh* means "the presence of sound." The song is saying that at that moment when the lute player stops, "the soundless wins over the sound" or "sound yields to silence." That space between notes is very, very powerful, very meaningful. It is more eloquent than any sound. The soundless can be more pleasant, more profound, than sound. Trinh Cong Son felt the same thing.

One of my American students shared with me similar

comments made by American saxophonist David Sanborn in an interview. Referring to his fellow saxophonist
Hank Crawford and the renowned composer-trumpeter
Miles Davis, Sanborn said: "[Hank] understood that
the space you leave is as important as the sound that you
make. . . . And then when I heard Miles Davis, I gravi-
tated to . . . his simplicity and his use of space [and not
having] to fill all those spaces."

## ananda and the music
## of relationships

Relationships and communication are also a kind of
music. Sitting with friends, you don't need to say anything. If you have understanding and can enjoy the true
presence you offer each other, that is enough. I am convinced that during those miserable years of the wars in
Vietnam, Trinh Cong Son's greatest consolation was the
quiet moments with his friends. But if a person doesn't
know how to sit like that, if he knows only how to pour
one alcoholic drink after another, then those kinds of
moments will never be available to him.

 One time when the Buddha was staying at the

Jetavana Monastery in India, while the two hundred resident monks were preparing for the annual rainy-season retreat, three hundred more monks arrived from Kosambi. The monks were all happy to see each other again and were talking together loudly. Hearing the noise from his room, the Buddha asked his senior disciple Shariputra, "What is all the commotion?"

Shariputra answered, "There are some brothers coming in from Kosambi; they're celebrating their reunion with a lot of loud chatter and losing their mindful manners. Please forgive them."

The Buddha said, "If they're going to be that raucous, they have to go elsewhere. They cannot stay here." The Buddha wanted to teach the monks about using their energy in more conscious and meaningful ways.

Shariputra announced to the monks what the Buddha had said. The monks quieted down and moved to another location nearby to have their rains retreat. Throughout those ninety days of retreat, the monks remembered what the Buddha had taught about not losing themselves in idle chatter. They culti-vated mindfulness and concentration wholeheartedly, and by the end of the retreat they had realized quite a lot of transformation. It's not that they had become heavy, serious, and solemn; in fact, their faces were brighter and their smiles were fresh.

At the conclusion of their retreat, the monks wanted to go back and thank the Buddha for his correction. When that news reached Shariputra, he told the Buddha, "Dear Teacher, the monks have finished their retreat and they want to pay their respects to you." The Buddha allowed the monks to come in, and he joined his palms in greeting.

It was about seven o'clock in the evening. Around three hundred monks from Kosambi, plus a couple hundred resident monks, sat with the Buddha in the big meditation hall. Teacher and students sat together in silence from seven o'clock until midnight, no one saying a word.

Ananda, the Buddha's attendant, went to the Buddha and said, "Dear respected Teacher, it's about midnight. Is there anything you want to tell the monks?" The Buddha did not reply; and they all continued like that until three o'clock in the morning, just sitting together without saying anything. The attendant Ananda was a bit perplexed, so he went again to the Buddha and said, "It's now three o'clock; is there anything you want to say to these monks?" But the Buddha just went on sitting in silence with everyone.

At five o'clock in the morning Ananda came again and insisted: "Dear Teacher, the sun is coming up. Aren't you going to say anything to the monks?"

The Buddha finally spoke. "What do you want me to say? Teacher and students, sitting together peacefully and happily like that—is it not enough?"

Simply being able to see and appreciate one another's presence was a very big happiness. Although the experience was without any sound, it was infinitely more valuable than any sound would have been.

## coming together in silence

In everyday life, many of us interact all day long with other people. With mindfulness, we can always tap into a refreshing inner solitude. As I mentioned earlier, solitude is not found only by being alone in a hut deep in the forest; it is not about cutting ourselves off from civilization, although that certainly is one type of spiritual retreat we can take.

*Real solitude comes from a stable*

*heart that does not get carried away*

*by the pull of the crowd, nor by*

*sorrows about the past, worries about*

*the future, or excitement or*

*stress about the present.*

———

We do not lose ourselves; we do not lose our mindfulness. Taking refuge in our mindful breathing, coming back to the present moment, is to take refuge in the beautiful, serene island that each of us has within.

We can enjoy being together with others without getting lost in emotions or latching onto perceptions. Instead, we can see the other people as our support. When we see someone who moves in mindfulness, speaks with love, and enjoys her or his work, this person is our reminder to return to our own source of mindfulness. When we see someone who is distracted and dispersed, this can be a bell of mindfulness as well, reminding us to be diligent in connecting with our true presence and offering that to ourselves and others. Perhaps the other person will pick up on our quality of presence and be encouraged to come back to herself as well.

When we enjoy our time with the people around us, and we don't feel lost in our interactions, then wherever we are, we can smile and breathe in peace, dwelling contentedly in the island of self.

Having a community of support for our regular practice is crucial. If we can have the opportunity to sit with other people and allow the collective energy of mindfulness to embrace our suffering, we are like a drop of water flowing in a vast river, and we feel much better.

*The most precious thing we can give*

*to one another is our presence, which*

*contributes to the collective energy*

*of mindfulness and peace.*

*We can sit for those who can't sit, walk for*

*those who can't walk, and create*

*stillness and peace within us for people*

*who have no stillness or peace.*

———

We may not have to do anything at all for the knots inside us to loosen and untie themselves in such an atmosphere.

Healing oneself and healing the world at the same time really is possible with every awakened step, with every awakened breath.

## developing collective habits

Collective consciousness can be a toxic food or a wholesome one. Collective habits of thought, speech, and action likewise can be either healthy or unhealthy. If we make a commitment together—as a group at work, or as a family, or with friends—to breathe mindfully before we answer the phone, or to stop and listen when we hear the sound of a bell, a phone ringing, a clock chiming, a siren, or a plane overhead, these become beneficial collective habits.

Collective habits can be very powerful. We can support one another to stop following old, unhealthy habits and go in a better direction. Together, we can stop our thinking and focus on our breathing. We can support each other to breathe in gently and concentrate on our in-breath, to breathe out gently and pay attention to our out-breath. This is something very simple to do, but its effect is great. If everybody stops the thinking, and breathes together with awareness, then automatically we are no longer isolated individuals; we are a joyful collective. We don't act as a collection of separate bodies; we act as a community, a super-organism. A new level of energy is generated that is even more powerful than the energy we produce when we mindfully breathe or walk by ourselves.

When we allow our body to relax and allow the collective energy of mindfulness and concentration to enter, healing can happen easily. When we have a frustration, opening our body and mind and allowing the collective energy of mindfulness and concentration to come in can be profoundly healing.

## nourishing others

We can learn how to generate a powerful and healing silence not only in our families or even our local practice groups, but also in our larger communities. If you are a schoolteacher, you should know how to nurture that kind of noble, refreshing silence in your class. If you are a business or community leader, you can propose beginning each meeting or each workday with this kind of silence.

When I was in India in 1997, I visited the president of the Parliament and I proposed to him that he introduce into legislative sessions the practice of listening to the bell, breathing, and smiling. I suggested that the members start each session with mindful breathing and listening to the bell. I recommended that every time the discussion got hot, when people weren't capable of listening to each other anymore, they could invite the bell to sound so that the whole assembly would stop talking and practice mindful breathing to calm themselves down before they began discussing and listening again. Ten days later, he formed an ethics committee to oversee that kind of civilized practice in the Parliament.

If we carve out little moments of spaciousness in the various activities of our lives for this kind of quiet, we open ourselves up to the ultimate freedom. We're no longer jostling for position or for fame in the hope that these things will make us happy. We can be happy *right now*. We can have peace and joy in this very moment. Even if we have been restless our whole life and we have only two minutes left before we die, in that time we can stop our thoughts, take mindful breaths, and find stillness and peace. But why wait until we're on our deathbed to become present and treasure the miracle of being alive?

# practice:
# sitting for the sake
# of sitting

Sometimes people say, "Don't just sit there; do some-thing!" They are urging action. But mindfulness prac-titioners often like to say, "Don't just do something; sit there!" Nonaction is, in fact, also action. There are people who don't seem to do much, but whose pres-ence is crucial for the well-being of the world. The quality of their presence makes them truly available to others and to life. Nonaction, for them, is doing some-thing. You may sometimes find yourself longing to sit and do nothing, yet when the opportunity presents itself, you may not know how to enjoy it.

That's largely because our society is very goal-oriented. We tend to always be going in a certain direction and having a particular aim in mind. Bud-dhism, on the other hand, has a certain respect for en-lightened "aimlessness." That teaching says you don't have to put something in front of you and run after it, because everything is already there inside you. The same is true with sitting. Don't sit in order to attain a goal. Each moment of sitting meditation brings you back to life. Whatever you are doing, whether it's watering the garden, brushing your teeth, or doing the dishes, see if you can do it in a way that is "aimless."

*It's okay to make a wish, to have an aim.*

*But we shouldn't allow it to become*

*something that prevents us from living*

*happily in the here and the now.*

———

Sitting in silence can be wonderfully aimless. You can also practice guided meditation in a way that is aimless. Here is a meditation that helps cultivate spontaneity, freshness, solidity, clarity, and spaciousness.

*Breathing in, I know I'm breathing in.*
*Breathing out, I know I'm breathing out.*
*(In. Out.)*

*Breathing in, I see myself as a flower.*
*Breathing out, I feel fresh.*
*(Flower. Fresh.)*

*Breathing in, I see myself as a mountain.*
*Breathing out, I feel solid.*
*(Mountain. Solid.)*

*Breathing in, I see myself as still water.*
*Breathing out, I reflect things as they are.*
*(Water. Reflecting.)*

*Breathing in, I see myself as space.*
*Breathing out, I feel free.*
*(Space. Free.)*

*Also from*

*Thich Nhat Hanh*

HarperOne
*An Imprint of* HarperCollins*Publishers*

_Also from_

_Thich Nhat Hanh_

JUL 0 2 2015